CIRCLE OF FORM

CIRCLE OF FORM

FORM AND CONTRAST IN ARCHITECTURE

THOMAS ARVID JAEGER

AALBORG UNIVERSITY PRESS

The circle of form
Form and contrast in architecture

1. Edition, 1. Print run, 2020

© The Author and Aalborg University Press, 2020

Layout & graphic design: Jonathan Arvid Jaeger & the Author.
Cover design: Designer BA(Hons) Jonthan Arvid Jaeger

Printed at Toptryk Grafisk ApS 2020

ISBN: 978-87-7210-289-4

The book is published with support from the Department of Architecture and Media Technology, Aalborg University.

Thanks to Associate Professor Peter Mandal Hansen, Aarhus School of Architecture, Professor Adrian Carter, Bond University and Associate professor Kaare Eriksen, Aalborg University, for their comments and discussions on the subjects of this book. Finding relevant pictures is always a challenge. A special thanks go to Designer Felicia Arvid Jaeger and Arch. M.A.A Benjamin Arvid Jaeger for their contributions and to my students for testing and feedback on the analysis model presented in this book. Finally, I want to express sincere gratitude to the blind peer reviewer of this book and my wife, Tina Jaeger, for her continuous support and competent opinions during the process of writing.

PEER REVIEWED

All rights reserved. No part of this book may be reprinted or reproduced or utilized in any form or by any electronic, mechanical, or other means, now known or hereafter invented, including photocopying and recording, or in any information storage or retrieval system, without permission in writing from the publishers, except for reviews and short excerpts in scholarly publications.

CONTENTS

INTRODUCTION 7

FORM AND OPPOSITIONS 11

CIRCLE OF FORM 21

THE ABSTRACT LANGUAGE OF THE STRAIGHT 31

THE ENGAGING LANGUAGE OF THE CURVE 51

MASS AND STRUCTURE 75

SEPARATE OR UNITE? 91

ANALYZING FORM AND CONTRASTS 109

APPENDIX 1 130

REFERENCES 134

Bridges Zollamtssteg. Wienna. Photo. B.A.J.

Straight and curved, the two contrasting elements in form.

The upper bridge combines these two oppositions clear and without much drama, but when the straight is a distinctive diagonal, as the lower bridge, the result is a dramatic composition.

The oblique line has some of the dynamics of the curve - but in an entirely different way.

INTRODUCTION

Circle of Form introduces oppositions as a method to explain and understand the aspects of form in architecture. Based on theoretical research on oppositions related to art, architecture, and design, the content has been transformed into a small illustrative book focused on practice. It is for students of architecture but hopefully written in a way so everyone interested in this subject can enjoy reading it.

Dividing things in oppositions is a method often used to determine the basic elements in complex systems. Our culture uses opposites on all levels: Within the law, a clear distinction between truth or false, guilty or not guilty is fundamental, in politics opposites define the socialist left and the conservative right in most democracies.

In art opposites also define the (interacting) basic elements, like e.g. the circle of colour and the definition of complementary colours, the language's vowels and consonants, the music's major and minor, harmony and dissonance, as well as the difference between the beat and rhythm. Artists have used this mindset for centuries because simplicity supports a clear artistic language and oppositions emphasize expression and interaction. Why not use the same tool to determine the basic elements of form and understand their interplay?

The psychologist and Nobel Prize winner Daniel Kahneman, explains our thinking as an ongoing fight and collaboration between two opposite types of thinking: thinking fast (intuitive) and thinking slow (logic). (Kahneman 2012). He argues, that intuitive (emotional based) fast thinking is used for decision making in far too many situations, where the complexity of the problem demands slow logic thinking. Nevertheless, we use it because it is fast and easy! The same pattern we see in many aesthetic judgements, where the intuitive judgement of taste has been favoured so much, but at the same time is the source for misunderstandings and frustrations in many discussions on art, architecture and design.

This book wants to implement some slow thinking on the architectural form because it takes time and effort to split a composition into pieces, to achieve a better understanding when reassembling the parts into a unified whole. The question is: are opposites able to decompose form and composition objectively, to find some common ground to discuss aesthetics? The answer is the same as with other complex problems: start with the beginning, try to find the essential principles. Previous research in oppositions (Arvid Jaeger 2019) demonstrated that the same type of thinking could isolate and determine the basic elements of form – and the opposition-thinking enabled to put these into a model: Circle of Form.

This book aims to demonstrate how this relatively narrow perspective on form makes sense to understand the complexity of form and composition concerning architecture. On the analytic level, this mindset will show to the reader an ability to split works of architecture into well-defined parts, creating a simple and clear understanding of form and their relations in a composition.

On a conceptual level, many architects use oppositions to define the general idea. On the practical level the model's definition of the basic types of form and their particular nature support the user in making coherent choices during a design process – just as the examples in the last part of the book show many famous architects have been doing through the ages. These examples demonstrate to the reader how good design is not something related exclusively to some intuitive, artistic intelligence – but also based on principles with a special kind of mindset and logic, we can understand and learn.

Explaining architecture with opposites has a history in a Danish context. The architect and theorist, Steen Eiler Rasmussen, used pairs of opposites as themes in his lectures and the famous book "Experiencing Architecture" (Rasmussen 1957). This book was THE introduction to study architecture in Denmark for decades. Rasmussen himself was introduced to this theme as a student at the Royal Academy of Fine Arts by his professor Carl Petersen. In 1919 Petersen gave a famous lecture on oppositions in architecture, later published in Arkitekten – the Danish magazine for architects. (Petersen 1920). Petersen claimed in his lecture that many talented artists failed in their work because they lacked insight into the nature and use of opposites in their work. Petersen called for further research on this. Now, 100 years later, this book on oppositions tries to answer this call.

THE SIGNIFICANT FEATURES OF THIS DESIGN ARE **OPPOSITES**:

A SOLID CORE VERSUS A SLENDER GRID

A CIRCULAR CLOCK VERSUS A RECTANGULAR BUILDING.

VERTICAL VERSUS HORIZONTAL.

COMPLEXITY AT THE TOP VERSUS SIMPLICITY BELOW.

A SENSE OF UNITY IS CREATED VIA **SIMILARITIES** IN MATERIALS AND REPETITIONS OF FORM.

Aarhus City Hall. Bell tower. Arch. Arne Jacobsen 1944. Photo: T.A.J.

FORM AND OPPOSITIONS

The starting point is our ability to think and see similarities and oppositions. Things can be more or less different. In form, oppositions are a particular way to be different; they are contrasts. Their relationship is tense, and sometimes we experience it as if a sort of magnetic tension occurs between the shapes. The excitement or drama is something we add to the experience. Similarities create a sense of harmonic unity; they bind things together, while contrasts create expression. Most artists know and use this knowledge because contrasts help to clarify the artistic language and dramatize the composition, whether it is literature, music, painting, sculpture, product design or architecture. Obviously, the philosophical and cognitive question is if contrasts really exist or if they just are something, we invent?

Form, function, materials, manufacturing processes, construction and artistic themes change frequently, and every cultural epoch has its characteristics, but the basic principles of thinking and perception do not change. Light and dark, straight and curved, movement and still, continue to be experienced so substantially diverse, that we call them opposites – just as Pythagoras did in his list of opposites from the 6. Century B.C. (Friis Johansen 1998). Therefore, it is worth taking time to study contrasts in form and finding out what they are and how they interact.

Naturally, our vision and the way we see things plays a central role. The prerequisite is our minds ability to distinguish one form from the other and tell the difference – or the similarity. The ability to distinguish is crucial, and among the absolute essential visual and cognitive tools, we have. We understand the visual world by observing differences in light and shadow, form and colour. Differences are our guide to visual perception. Think about how dense fog makes us get totally lost. Similarities, on the other hand, bind things together, create patterns, groups and establish a sense of unity. We group things and establish connections. Similarities easily form coherence; just think about symmetry and repetitions.

Taking a closer look at the 3-dimensional form, we realize how oppositions define various elements of form: vertical and horizontal, straight and curved, concave and convex, massive and structural, light and heavy, coarse and fine, symmetry and asymmetry, simple and complex.

Defining elements of form with oppositions is nothing new. William Hogarth, the English painter, published in 1753 the book "The Analysis of Beauty" in which he tried to come to the core of what lies behind beauty – in nature and art. On the front of the book is a triangular glass prism with an s-shaped "serpentine" shaped line depicted inside – standing on a shelf with the inscription Variation. In the introduction, Hogarth writes in the preface that with this book he wishes to prove "that the triangular form of the glass and the serpentine line itself are the most expressive figures that can be thought of to signify not only beauty and grace but the whole order of form." Hogarth named the s-line "the line of beauty" and the serpentine line "the line of grace". (Hogarth 1753) In the late 19.cent. the famous art historian Heinrich Wölfflin developed a method using oppositions as an analytic tool to describe the differences between various periods in art and architecture. He presented this method in "Classic Art" (1899). Oppositions are "opposite poles, between which the artistic spirit oscillates" as Herbert Read later describes his approach in the preface to Wölfflin's book. (Wölfflin 1994)

Johannes Itten's revolutionary method of teaching art and design without focusing on styles transforms these ideas about design principles into a teaching method. He used oppositions as a systematic tool to define basic form and form related phenomenon's in his famous design course at the Bauhaus School 1921-23. Itten's basic form was 3 types of opposites: vertical/horizontal, oblique and curved. (Singer Bauhaus Archiv). Not only Itten but also Kandinsky used the opposites in his Bauhaus teaching. His approach to defining the basic elements of painting was also 3 types of opposites: "punkt, linie, fläche", point, line and plane. (Kandinsky 1923) Compared to Itten's, they had a different character and focused on the extension of form.

Fifty years later the perceptual psychologist Rudolf Arnheim used oppositions to define a broad spectrum of the basic principles of form in his book "The Dynamics of Architectural Form". He asked the following question:" How can one hope to realize what distinguishes the experience of the Parthenon in the Athens of the fifth century B.C. from that of a gothic cathedral in the Bourges of A.D. 1300 if one has no clear notion of the dynamic relations between vertical and horizontal?" (Arnheim 1977). "Dynamic relations" is another way of describing visual tensions between opposites.

However, neither of them created a system, or model, able to define, organize and differentiate the oppositions for systematic use in design practice. Hogarth, Itten and Arnheim defined the same basic forms, like vertical, horizontal, oblique and curved. Kandinsky did not focus on form, but his opposites described another vital aspect: its extension.

Modern research into the subject of perception of form has combined it with neuroscience – because it is possible measure the activities of the brain when confronted with different types of visual stimuli. In 1992 the Italian researcher Giacomo Rizzolatti found in experiments with monkeys that brain cells in the frontal lobes activate in the same way by looking as by doing an action itself. It is common knowledge that humans have developed extraordinary skills in fast and very accurate reading of curves in faces and are able immediately to tell us what a person feels. Studies on monkeys have shown that the centre reading curves are situated close to the centre of facial recognition. So it is perhaps not so strange that we have an exceptional relation to curves and research indicates that humans develop an early preference for curves. (Gómez-Puerto, Gerardo et al. 2016).

Our cognitive interaction with straight lines is very different. Often, in nature, they are connected to danger like zig-zag lines and repeated parallel lines. However, humans have used abstract geometric patterns with straight lines for thousands of years on every scale from architecture to jewellery but often mixed with decorative ornaments. Perhaps because these patterns appeal to our slow logic thinking?

Research by an English professor A.J. Wilkins demonstrates we use much more energy to process the visual scenes in a modernistic rectangular urban environment is much harder for the brain to process than in natural environment because of their repetitive rectangular patterns. (Wilkins, A.J. Le, T.D 2017). The straight lines in Eisenmann's Memorial in Berlin (p.126) tell us something about what the excessive use of simple concrete geometric forms can communicate: the feeling of cold and fear. Nevertheless, we find the same type of form and material used in facades of Fuksas Church in Foligno (p.116), where the purpose is quite the opposite.

Of course, these examples are only a fragment of the enormous research conducted in this area. However, they indicate that science is on its way to give us a much better insight into how perception, logic thinking, feelings and form interact. A more detailed discussion on this subject is in Contrasts/Modsætninger (Arvid Jaeger 2019).

Science cannot solve the artistic problems of creating form because it is a discipline one has to practice.

In Danish it is called "formgivning": the process of giving form (to something). It is about the challenging skill to develop motives, expression and meaning in form. It is how we control the similarity and difference; how we put them together and place them against each other with varying strength, creating a sense of unity using diversity.

Artistic processes rely on intuitive and rational decision-making during the design process as Donald Schön called "reflection in action" (Schön 1983) and opposites are one of the tools to make choices. They simplify, clarify and speed up this process. The same pattern of opposite thinking we find on more abstract levels in the creative process: in concept development related to architecture and design, we typically use terms like traditional versus radical; integration versus difference, passive versus active, form versus function, public versus private etc.

This book does not advocate or favour any particular kind of aesthetics.However, it offers a way to see, experience and discuss form in a composition - hopefully on a more elaborated level.

This short introduction implies how form theory is a rather complex hybrid between quantitative and qualitative aspects of form, supported by theories of perception, cognition, neuroscience and more phenomenological theories from practice in art and architecture.

Those readers wishing to study further see the references on the last page.

Notre Dame du Haut 1955. Arch. Le Corbusier. Photo: B.A.J.

The concrete outdoor pulpit illustrates the dynamic relations between oppositions in form, texture, light and shadow. Le Corbusier used a variety of contrasts to evoke the significant expression of the chapel in Ronchamps.

THINK SIMILAR

SIMILARITIES ARE AN INTEGRAL PART OF THE WAY WE THINK. THEY MAKE US SEE PATTERNS AND CONNECTIONS BETWEEN DIVERSE THINGS.

IN FORM, SIMILARITY CREATES A SENSE OF UNITY. SIMILARITY, KNOWN AS REPETITION OR SYMMETRY, IS OFTEN CALLED HARMONY.

SIMILARITIES CREATE VISUAL ORDER. IF NOT CONTROLLED, THEY WILL RESULT IN ENDLESS REPETITIONS AND MONOTONY.

THINK OPPOSITE

MOST FORMS ARE JUST DIFFERENT, BUT SOME HAVE A SPECIAL RELATIONSHIP – THEY ARE OPPOSITES.

OPPOSITES ARE AN INTEGRAL PART OF THE WAY WE THINK. THEY DEFINE EACH OTHER AND MAKE THINGS CLEAR.

CLEAR VISUAL OPPOSITES ARE CONTRASTS.

IN FORM, CONTRASTS CREATE CLARITY, TENSION AND DRAMA. IF NOT CONTROLLED, THEY CAUSE VISUAL DISTORTION AND CHAOS.

Pantheon in Rome. Photo: T.A.J.

CIRCLE OF FORM

**GEOMETRIC STRAIGHT AND ORGANIC CURVED
MASS AND STRUCTURE
THE 4 BASIC ELEMENTS OF FORM**

CIRCLE OF FORM

The Circle of Form is an illustrative model, setting the basic types of form and their similarity and contrast effects into a system. Its starting point is the two types of shape: straight-lined and curved form – and because it focuses on 3-dimensional form, adds the extent: mass/volume and structure/void. In a model of basic form it is essential to arrange the elements into the right categories – so the model does not mix compositional elements like asymmetry and symmetry with basic elements like concave and convex.

The general terms Geometric and Organic refer to the fact that any form consists of straight or curved lines/surfaces – or various combinations of these, hybrids, like, e.g. a cone or a cylinder, which combines straight and curved form.

The terms Mass and Structure refer to the fact that physical form either is emerging with a closed continuous surface, as volume/mass or with an open split surface, as grid/structure with voids or various transformations of these. This pair of opposites represents the object and the void. In the extreme version, Mass is a solid form with no structure or offsets in the surfaces. The extreme version of Structure is an empty void.

On the quantitative level, the rectilinear forms and the curved forms define two significantly different types. They are contrasts. Therefore these are placed opposite each other. The related forms are next to each other. They transform stepwise, like graduations, between Mass and Structure. The most significant contrast effects we find, of course, where disparities are most significant: massive-geometric has a significantly greater contrast to structural-organic form than solid-geometric form has to solid-organic. Solid-organic form creates a contrast to structural-organic form but is of obviously even more in contrast to structural-geometric form. In this model, forms including both the straight and the curved lines, for example, cylinders, cones, single curved form or the like, shall be considered blended or hybrid forms. In these, one type of form modifies or mixes with its opposition. Mixed forms belong to the central area of the model. In the middle, if the opposites equal or to one side, depending on whether curved or straight dominates. The cylinder is one of the most popular types of hybrid forms, perhaps because it is the perfect compromise: straight and curved, hard and soft at the same time.

On the qualitative level, the description of the two types of form enables the reader to understand the qualities of expression connected to curved and straight – and what happens, when we combine them. Knowledge about the real difference of how we perceive these opposites is the basis of the qualitative terms linked to the two types of form. This insight has the potential to make us much more aware of the language of form. How we use it, communicate with it and use it to create different kinds of moods.

On the one hand, The Circle of Form is a simple analytic model making it possible to understand form and composition by identifying the basic types of form and their interrelationships. On the other hand, the model is a creative design tool.

Whether we are talking about simple or complex compositions, the Circle of Form facilitate the process of making coherent, aesthetic choices. By focusing on being similar or opposite, the model introduces extreme thinking in the design process. Hopefully, this will increase clarity as well as vitality in the design.

Thinking similar and opposite is a mindset, which the reader must work out through the mind and develop through the practice of the eye. The reader will not become a great artist by studying the laws of contrast, but hopefully a far more competent professional. So, mastering form and aesthetics is not only a matter of intuition, feeling, sensation and personal taste. It is also a matter of knowing how it works.

The Circle of Form is a very simplified model and describes far from all phenomenons related to the complex world of forms. In a design process, one must apply many other design-related parameters. However, many of these described with pairs of opposites, such as:

symmetry - asymmetry, high - low, big, small,
closed - open, narrow - wide, repetition - variation,
rest - movement, light - dark, classic - modern,
recognizeable - abstract, inviting - dismissive......

These pairs of opposites are not types of form. They are typically included as additional "layers", creating difference or similarity on other levels of in a composition.

Finally, we must accept the general understanding of the central concepts, geometric and organic has different professional and cultural codes embedded. Therefore, when discussing form, it can often be more comfortable and more precise to use the basic terms, defining geometric as straight and organic as curved.

CIRCLE OF FORM
BASIC TYPES OF FORM AND MEANING

ORGANIC	GEOMETRIC
Engaging dynamics from curves	Abstraction from straight lines

QUANTITATIVE PROPERTIES

CURVED
CONCAVE
CONVEX
SPIRAL
WAVE
CIRCLE
OVAL
SPHERE
PARABOLA
HYPERBOLA
EGGFORM
LEAFFORM

EMOTIONAL
ENGAGING
INTUITIVE
CONTINUOUS
MOVEMENT
WARM
SOFT

QUALITATIVE PROPERTIES

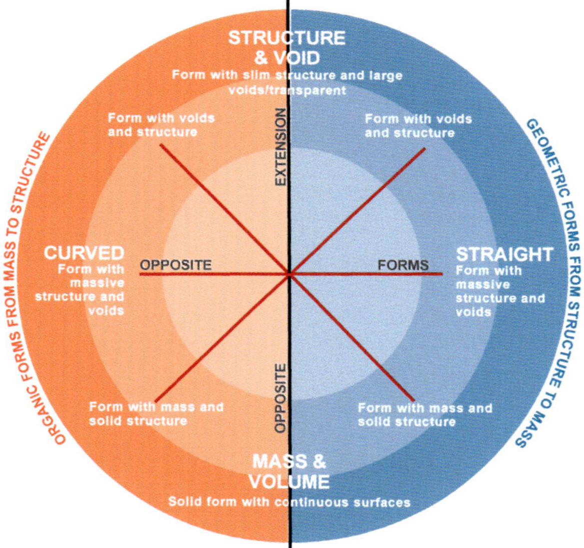

QUANTITATIVE PROPERTIES

STRAIGHT
VERTICAL
HORIZONTHAL
OBLIQUE
SQUARE
RECTANGULAR
TRIANGULAR
TRAPEZ
PLANE
CUBE
PYRAMID
CRYSTALLINE

LOGIC
ABSTRACT
RATIONAL
SEQUENTIAL
STILL
COLD
HARD

QUALITATIVE PROPERTIES

Central diagram:
- **STRUCTURE & VOID**: Form with slim structure and large voids/transparent
- **CURVED**: Form with massive structure and voids — OPPOSITE — **STRAIGHT**: Form with massive structure and voids
- **MASS & VOLUME**: Solid form with continuous surfaces
- Form with voids and structure (both sides)
- Form with mass and solid structure (both sides)
- EXTENSION / OPPOSITE FORMS
- ORGANIC FORMS FROM MASS TO STRUCTURE
- GEOMETRIC FORMS FROM STRUCTURE TO MASS

Ill. Th. Arvid Jaeger

CIRCLE OF FORM
OPPOSITIONS OF FORM AND MASS
TRANSFORMATIONS OF FORM AND MASS

ORGANIC
Engaging dynamics from curves

GEOMETRIC
Abstraction from straight lines

ORGANIC FORMS FROM MASS TO STRUCTURE

GEOMETRIC FORMS FROM STRUCTURE TO MASS

STRUCTURE & VOID
Form with slim structure and large voids/transparent

Form with voids and structure

Form with voids and structure

CURVED
Form with massive structure and voids

OPPOSITE

FORMS

STRAIGHT
Form with massive structure and voids

EXTENSION

OPPOSITE

Form with mass and solid structure

Form with mass and solid structure

MASS & VOLUME
Solid form with continuous surfaces

Ill. Th. Arvid Jaeger

CIRCLE OF FORM
BASIC FORMS ALONG THE PERIPHERY
HYBRID FORMS TOWARDS THE CENTER

ORGANIC
Engaging dynamics from curves

GEOMETRIC
Abstraction from straight lines

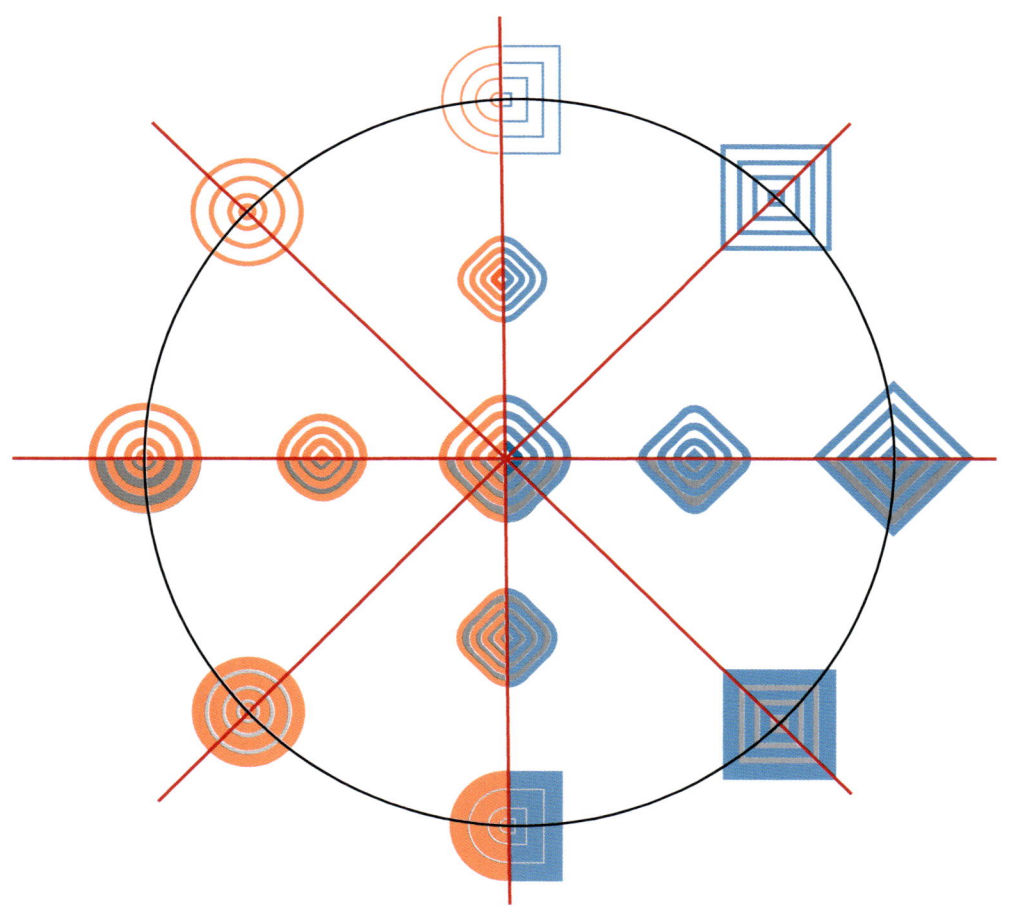

Ill. Th. Arvid Jaeger

CIRCLE OF FORM
EXAMPLES FROM ARCHITECTURE
In "organic" architecture straight lines are common.
In "geometric" architecture curves are the exeption.

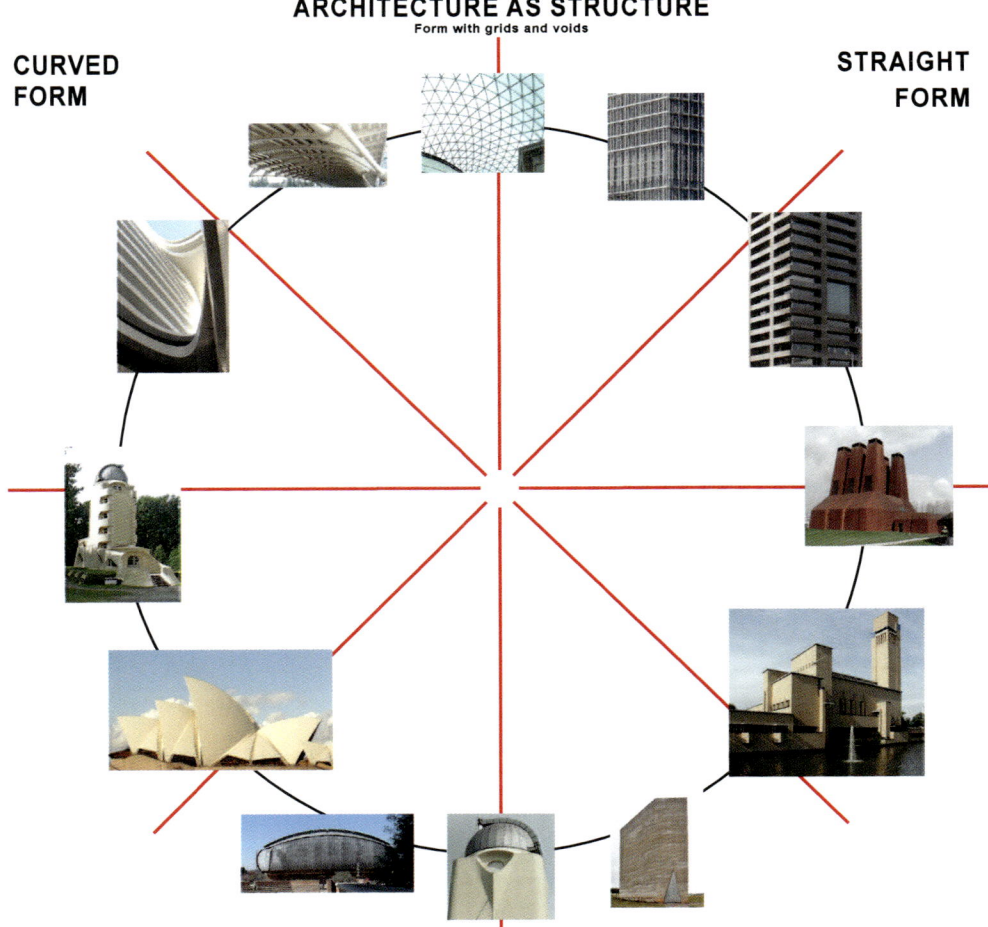

Ill. Th. Arvid Jaeger

DEFINING FORM

FORM IS SHAPED BY STRAIGHT OR CURVED LINES AND SURFACES – OR A MIX OF THESE.

FORM CAN APPEAR WITH A CONTINUOUS SURFACE, AS VOLUME/ MASS OR WITH AN OPEN DISCONTINUED SURFACE, AS GRID/STRUCTURE WITH VOIDS.

THE QUALITY OF THE STRUCTURE IS ITS ABILITY TO MAKE THE FORM APPEAR LIGHT AND TRANSPARENT. THE QUALITY OF THE MASS IS ITS ABILITY TO MAKE THE FORM APPEAR SOLID AND HEAVY.

IN SMALL SCALE STRUCTURE AND MASS RELATE TO PATTERN AND TEXTURE ON THE SURFACE.

DEFINING SHAPE

THE CIRCLE OF FORM DIVIDES SHAPES INTO TWO CATEGORIES: CURVED AND STRAIGHT, I.E. ORGANIC AND GEOMETRIC.

THE QUALITY OF THE CURVES ARE THEIR ABILITY TO ENGAGE. THE QUALITY OF THE STRAIGHT LINES ARE THEIR ABILITY TO ABSTRACT.

FORMS COMBINING STRAIGHT AND CURVED, SUCH AS A CYLINDER, A CONE OR IN OTHER WAYS BLEND STRAIGHT AND CURVED IS DEFINED AS MIXED OR HYBRID FORMS.

A STRAIGHT LINE OR SURFACE RESTRAIN THE MOTION OF THE CURVE. A CURVED LINE OR SURFACE ADDS MOTION TO THE STRAIGHT.

THE ABSTRACT LANGUAGE OF
THE STRAIGHT

Castel Vecchio. Verona. Arch. Carlo Scarpa 1959-73. Photo: B.A.J.

WHAT IS
GEOMETRIC FORM?

Most people can distinguish between straight linear and curved shape. The straight lines or shapes define a particular "section" in the world of forms and often called Geometric. The variety of shapes unfold between right-angled and oblique. The geometric form is cubical, crystalline and abstract. Herein lies its paramount quality. We find its natural reference in the lifeless world of mineral crystals. Its abstract quality is the ability to be "unnatural".
Modern architecture in glass and concrete is for many people the most common reference to geometric form. Geometric form often occurs in contexts using terms such as logic, rational, order, system. It has a rational atmosphere and links to principles in mathematics.

THE REDUCTION OF ALL KINDS TO THE MOST SIMPLE GEOMETRIC PRINCIPLES IS THE ESSENTIAL BASIS FOR A NEW AND ORIGINAL BEGINNING.
Eric Mendelsohn, 1923

The radical style of functionalism at the beginning of the 20th century changed architecture and challenged both the decorative styles and the classical tradition. However, the avant-garde did preserve some connections to the past. The students at the Bauhaus studied handcraft and old masters in painting and Johannes Itten's "Formenlehre", that reduced the diversity of form to a few simple, basic principles: Vertical/horizontal/cubic forms. Oblique/triangular forms. Curved/circular forms. Two types are geometric, one organic.

Many Cubist works are not "cubic" but "crystalline", because the images and sculptures are broken into facetted surfaces and forms. A common goal for many of these avant-garde movements was the desire to express a "new objectivity" in form, creating a new abstract idiom, freed from nature and traditions. The Dutch "De Stijl manifesto" spoke of a new plastic art "eliminating" al natural form and De Stijl painter Piet Mondrian worked solely with vertical and horizontal lines, rectangles and squares.

These statements belong of course to a certain period, but explain very well the general perception of geometric form. In this context, geometric form defines forms, made by straight lines or surfaces: straight rods, straight planes/ sheets, straight grids and solids such as cubes, triangles, rectangles, diamonds and crystals. This definition follows the tradition of Plato and his five geometric solids. In everyday speech, we call many other forms geometric, e.g. circles, spheres and cylinders.

VERTICAL & HORIZONTAL

Some say that all forms, curved and straight, are geometric because it is possible to describe them mathematically. Therefore, we need to clarify the concepts: Only shapes and structures made by the straight-lined or plain surfaces, belong to the geometric world. Shapes combining straight with curved, such as a cylinder, a cone or a single curved waveform represent a mix between geometric and organic forms, are hybrids. They combine the "hard" with the "soft" in a precise and straightforward form.

The square is the most simple rectangular shape. The ratio between horizontal and vertical is 1:1. The rectangle is more unbalanced and slightly "dynamic". The difference between the two directions determines how "dynamic" the rectangle is. When the differences increase – the rectangle becomes extreme.

The geometric, straight-lined form transforms itself between the massive, voluminous-like and the structural, skeleton-like: between Mass and Structure.
Horizontal-vertical shapes simplify the complex world and make things abstract. They easily create a sense of stillness and order – even though the relationship between vertical and horizontal is dramatic because they are oppositions.

VERTICAL AND HORIZONTAL DEFINE A SIMPLE ABSTRACT UNIVERSE. DUE TO THE SIMILARITIES IN LENGTHS, THE SQUARE BECOMES MORE STATIC THAN THE RECTANGULAR.

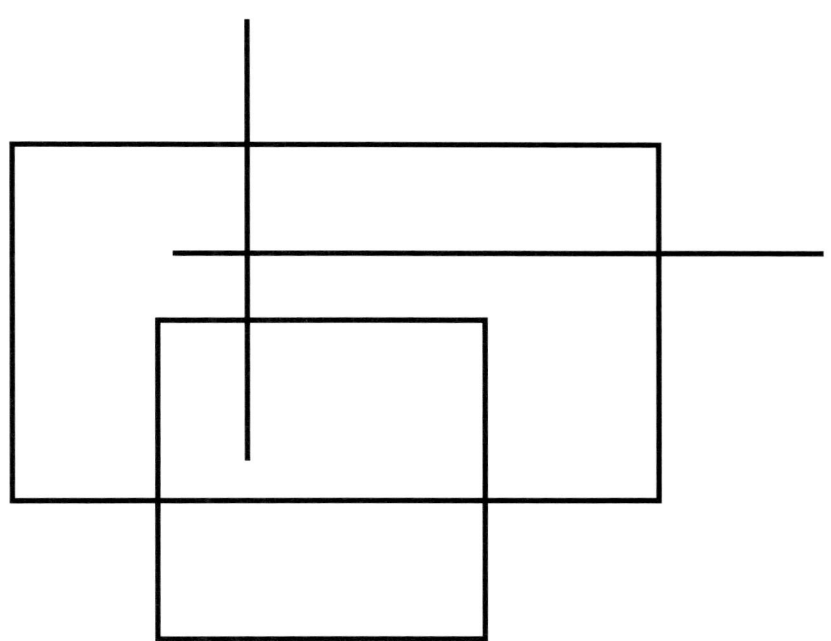

Town Hall Hilversum. 1924-31. Arch. M. Dudok. Photo: T.A.J.

Entrance door. Appartment bloc. Amsterdam. Photo: T.A.J.

The City Hall is a composition with emphasis on vertical and horizontal, in a solid geometric volume. Shifts and overlaps in a homogeneous brick building create a complex composition – without becoming chaotic. Most of the rectangular forms have extreme proportions: long and narrow. The window structure is a simple repetition of squares. The oblique elements are few: small horizontal balconies.

Even though it is a simple building, the variety of differences in sizes, offsets and directions give the solid volume a double expression: simple but complex, massive and structural at the same time.

In contrast to the brick walls surrounding it, this delicate wooden entrance becomes an extension of the interior of the house.

The symmetrical and horizontal offsets of this otherwise closed entrance set focus on the main door to the apartment block. Pushing the entrance forward creates a sense of invitation to move backwards, towards the door. The horizontal lines of letterboxes emphasize this expression. The stepped entrance facade appears hard and abstract, but the material makes us experience it warm and interior-like.

Orthogonal shapes: order and clarity.
The inner court of the Thermal Baths is a massive geometric universe in chilly grey stone contrasted with a fragile structure of handrails and poles of showers in warm golden brass. The abstract geometric forms create a dramatic contrast to the sloping organic landscape and frame the views of the mountains. Horizontal layers, recall walls to a quarry so, the basic structure of the building appears as if cut out of the rock. This sense of similarity links the building to the site. In this perspective, the orthogonal forms look significantly more dynamic than when seen from the front. However, the orthogonal system is simple, and maintains the impression of order and clarity.

Thermal Bath in Vals. 1996. Arch. Peter Zumthor Photo: B.A.J.

OBLIQUE

Oblique easily creates dynamics and is the one element in the geometric form most closely related to the dynamics of the organic – without being organic. It's "movement" is restricted and stiff – sometimes called "frozen". Compared to the logic and rational order of vertical/horizontal, the oblique distinguishes itself as being able to create chaos and feelings. Not the engaging feelings of the curve but the opposite.
The fragmented sticky character of some types of oblique shapes, make them look crystalline or even splintered and gives the impression of something aggressive, hard and cold. The Saha Hadid fire station in Vitra has this kind of expression. The pyramid, on the other hand, has an expression of an immoveable solid crystal.
In the vertical plane, oblique forms are out of balance. They are dynamic and demand our attention. It lies deep within us to be vigilant if something appears to be overturning. The leaning tower of Pisa is world-famous for the same reason.

Orthogonal and oblique have a tense relationship. Therefore, one can describe the relationship between right-angled and oblique, as a contrast between balance and imbalance, still and movement – knowing that "movement" in the geometric world is something relatively rigid or stiff – quite different from the sweeping movement of a curve.
The impression of movement is also present when the offset of orthogonal rectangles/cubic forms are creating an imaginative, oblique line or curve. If the cubic forms further-

more are tilted, the impression of instability and movement increases.

The oblique line brings dynamic into the otherwise static, right-angled world and therefore connect effortlessly to curves without stopping the motion. Because oblique can be different in many directions, no one can determine the slope of an oblique line by eye with the same accuracy as the vertical and horizontal ones. Perhaps this is why we have difficulties in finding an order, a pattern.

Hence, oblique is more subjective, free, dialectic and we find this type of form connected to the style of expressionism.

Compositions with different angles of oblique are the easy way to create dynamism, complexity and chaos – but creates steady stability, if they spread out downwards. The most elementary oblique shape is the triangle; a very dynamic figure compared to the horizontal/vertical rectangle.

The triangle can both seem stable or unstable, depending on whether it stands at the tip or the base. The outward sloping shape provides a movement downwards and experience of heaviness and extra stability, while the reverse form creates an impression of weightless and instability. Thus, oblique is incredibly exciting but often demanding and challenging to work within a composition.

Actelion Centre 2010. Arch. Herzog de Meuron. Photo B.A.J.

Helvetia Insurance. St. Gallen 2004. Arch. Herzog de Meuron. Photo BAJ

The oblique lines bring dynamic to the otherwise static, right-angled world. The Actelion Centre has traditionally horizontal floors and vertical walls – but because the volumes of the office spaces are an oblique structure and the expression immediately becomes complex and chaotic. This perspective view from the ground makes it even more dramatic. The diagonal columns add to the chaotic gesture. Oblique lines are an effective way to create complexity and chaos.

A variety of tilting offsets of the glass panels in this otherwise strict geometric facade, brake the coherence of the system.

The reflections create a surprising, chaotic effect compared to a traditionally mounted glass facade. The same tilting effect is common in older houses with single glazed bar windows, although much smaller in scale.

45

Heating central Utrecht 2005. Arch. Liesbeth v. d. Pol.

Oblique forms can create two opposite expressions: dynamic instability and firm stability.
These buildings with outward and downward sloping structures provide the last type of experience
The boiler house transforms three crystalline volumes into a robust structure of six pyramid chimneys.

The Tate Modern combines the dynamics of oblique with the stability of horizontal. These introduce a rigid contrasting structure and a sense of order in the dramatic, tilting architectural landscape of bricks.
The asymmetric oblique fold of the otherwise symmetric looking volume of the Tate adds extra dynamics to the composition.
On the top, a massive rooftop elevated on a contrasting void with a vertical structure, finishes the building.

OBLIQUE OFFSET

OFFSETS CREATE AN IMPRESSION OF OBLIQUE OR EVEN MAKE A "STEPPED CURVE".
TILTING OFFSETS INCREASE THE IMPRESSION OF DYNAMICS AND MOTION.

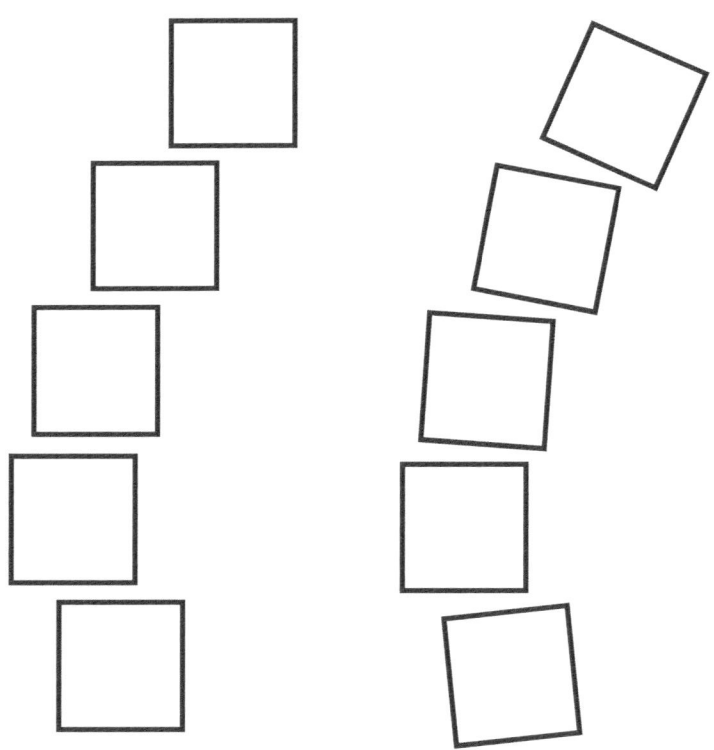

OBLIQUE FORM

OBLIQUE CREATES A CRYSTALLINE AND CHAOTIC TYPE OF FORM.
OBLIQUE GENERATE AN IMPRESSION OF "STIFF MOTION" AND DYNAMICS IN THE GEOMETRIC UNIVERSE.

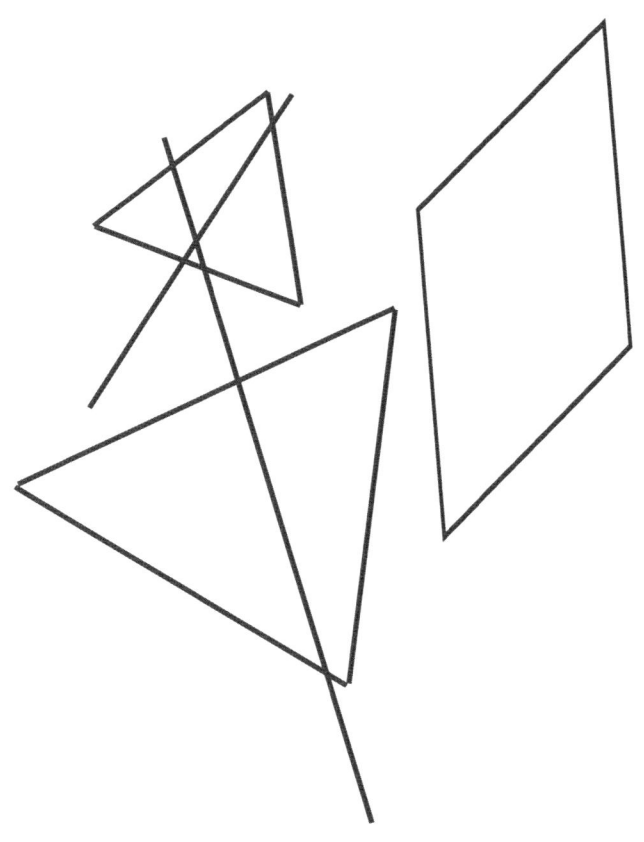

GEOMETRIC FORM

TYPES OF FORM:

SQUARE, TRIANGLE, RECTANGLE, RHOMBUS, TRAPEZOID, PENTAGON, HEXAGON, CRYSTALLINE.

BASIC ELEMENTS: VERTICAL, HORIZONTAL, OBLIQUE. PLANAR OR STRAIGHT SURFACE.

STILL: VERTICAL AND HORIZONTAL

MOTION: OBLIQUE LINES AND FORMS GENERATE AN IMPRESSION OF "STIFF MOTION" AND DYNAMICS.

OFFSETS OF VERTICAL/HORIZONTAL CREATE AN IMPRESSION OF OBLIQUE OR EVEN MAKE A "STEPPED CURVE".

GEOMETRIC SHAPES

Galaxy SOHO. Being 2012. Zaha Hadid Architects. Photo B.A.J.

THE ENGAGING LANGUAGE OF
THE CURVE

WHAT IS
ORGANIC FORM?

What is particular about organic form?

When Heraclitus said "everything flows", it is a truth more extensive than one immediately expected, related to the organic world. Nature's shape and fluid forms have a lot in common. We see traces of flow forms everywhere in living nature. It is perhaps not so strange when a jellyfish has this mark. Still, it is probably more surprising that characteristic flow forms show up in the structure of flower pistils, in animal horns, as well as in the solid bones of animals and humans.

In the Circle of Form, the term organic is not only used to describe forms from nature but as a common terminology for all curved shapes, surfaces and lines.

The curved universe is very dissimilar to the geometric one. The first difference between geometric and organic is that organic shape often has an apparent and direct reference to living nature. The second difference is that curved form has tensions and dynamics and far more direct access to our emotions. Organic form links to our experience of movement and life in a way, we do not find in any straight-lined geometric form.

For this reason, we often use emotional terms and terms from nature to describe organic form, even when the shapes become abstract. Therefore, it is a challenge to work with organic form, if we want to avoid all kinds of straightforward associations with natural forms.

This similarity implies that non-figurative organic form must be treated with far more care than geometric form – to remain abstract. A car looking like a turtle, or a water kettle looking like a fish, a milk pot in the shape of a cow soon becomes a joke. We know the method from cartoons, children's books and amusement parks. They use this excessively and quite deliberately because somehow we find this mingling between form and expression funny.

Even if abstraction often is preferable concerning architecture, we must acknowledge the artistic quality in the right balance between abstraction and metaphoric recognition. Well-chosen metaphors often add an extra dimension of meaning to architecture and design.

Jørn Utzon's Sydney Opera House exemplifies this brilliantly, with its organic shells on the geometric podium. The metaphors we imagine give us a key to the understanding and support creating unique architectual identity, which a purely abstract form is unable to deliver.

The Sydney Opera House belongs to a small group of unique, organic buildings created during the 1950s. The Opera House is something special, not only because of Jørn Utzon's artistic idea.
He designed the project based on a sophisticated knowledge of organic form originating from his passion for yacht design and construction, where organic shapes are the rule instead of the exception. His desire to solve the challenging aesthetic and constructive problems in a sublime interaction between form and construction have the origins in this tradition.
The convex shells of the Opera House are flat-faced outside and have strong structural ribs inside. The glass protruding from the inside of the domes

has a strong rib structure too. It is a dualistic composition in which Utzon uses straight and curved to emphasize and control one another.

Repetition and transformation, both in size and inclination, emphasizes the organic expression. Between the domes are transitional forms linking the shells together. They are cut straight at the bottom, creating oblique openings for windows behind. Even though the static geometric base forms a strong contrast to the shells, the diagonal steps elevating the podium towards the sea interacts with the straight oblique lines of domes above. Sydney Operahouse. 1957-. Arch. Jørn Utzon.

Sydney Opera. 1957- Arch. J. Utzon.Photo:T.A.J.

The intersection between the domes of the opera shows the fascinating dynamics of the sweeping curve, designed by Utzon with contrasting sharp edges and geometric patterns. The patterns are strictly geometric but with oblique lines and offsets supporting the impression of movement.

The signature of flow form and its sweeping curves embodies a high degree of continuity - no straight lines or surfaces, but instead a variety of convex and concave. Even though round surfaces of a body gives a soft expression we find sharp edges between concave and convex forms – like the picture to the left – defining the meeting of curved surfaces with exactness.

An edge adds sharpness and control to the organic flow, just as the meaning "giving an edge" to something indicates. However, organic form is challenging to work with because of the movement. Its connection to our feelings comes with a price. It quickly becomes swollen, sloppy, vulgar, chaotic and creates feelings of distaste or even nausea.

Controlling curved form takes time to learn because its lines and shapes are sensitive. Adding straight lines and surfaces help to manage the dynamics of the curves.

Terms describing organic form are; flowing, moving, living, tension, transformation, sensitivity to the context and unity in form and material. However, in otherwise geometric compositions, we can experience the organic, if composed according to the organic principles of movement and transformation. It combines repetition with variation without destroying the pattern - an "elastic" universe in contrast to the stiff geometric.

When an arc is combined with its mirror image, concave and convex occur.

The interaction between the two opposites, concave and convex, is essential and tells us a lot about the unique nature of the organic form – particularly if we compare this to the interaction between the basic, geometric forms. A convex surface leaping forward is active and engages with the viewer. A body forming a void inward gives way for you is concave. It is not passive, but active in the opposite way of the convex – something like pressure and vacuum. In other words, concave and convex can achieve a dynamic dialogue with their surroundings. Where concave, hollow surfaces intersect, they form sharp edges and even become sticky (like thorns). Convex forms fill, invade and occupy space. When they are round and soft; we experience them friendly, but when having sharp edges from concave, they might become aggressive. In between these two extremes lies the plain flat surface in a state of equilibrium. It is neutral.

CONCAVE, CONVEX, S-LINE AND SPIRAL DEFINE THE BASIC ELEMENTS OF THE ORGANIC UNIVERSE – FULL OF TENSION AND MOVEMENT

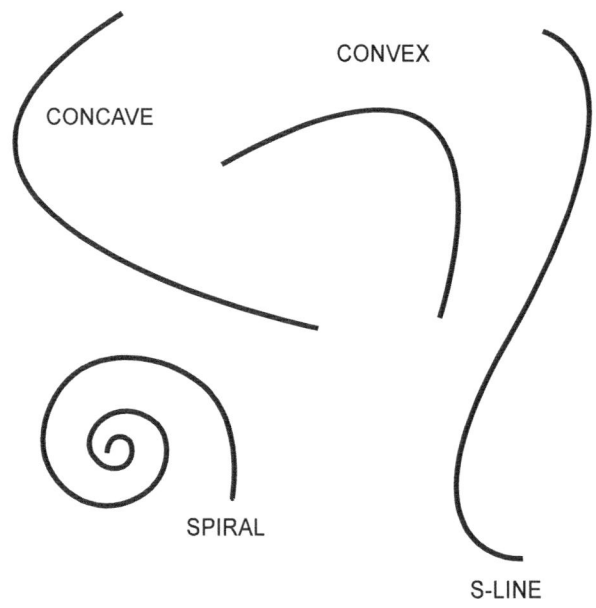

Meeting room. DZ Bank. 1999 Berlin. Arch. Frank Gehry. Photo: T.A.J

A double-curved surface is a surface curving in two directions/planes.
It represents the essence of organic form. With its undulating double-curved form, we experience it as filled with movement and dynamics - even though it is absolute stationery.
"Hard" metal plates cover the "soft" surface with oblique straight lines in an irregular pattern supporting its undulating movement - the opposite strategy of the building illustrated on the next page.

Solid looking convex and concave.
Curved forms have a unique ability to make hard materials seem soft. This massive double-curved structure clad with semi-matt grey metal panels has a surprisingly smooth and friendly expression - which should almost be impossible to achieve in this scale and these materials.
The concave cavities of this monumental city space invite people to sit in the shade around its base. Concave and convex can achieve a dialogue with the surrounding area.

The Dongdaemun Design Plaza. 2014. Seoul. Saha Hadid Architects. Photo T.A.J

CIRCLE & OVAL

The circle is something special in the organic world. It is curved and yet without movement because of its total symmetry. Its perfect balance and the total symmetry repeal movement. Although we tend to perceive the circle or the sphere as an abstract (unnatural) form, both are an integrated part of the organic world: in the circular waves erupting from a drip in the water, the eye, flowers, seeds or the sphere of umbels on dandelions, thistles and onion flowers, etc. A circle has the same simple defined geometry, which otherwise characterizes the elementary geometric forms. The circle or sphere then somehow becomes the organic pendant to the geometric square and cube.

The oval, on the other hand, is significantly different from the circle. An oval has no fixed geometry: there are many variants of ovals - just like the rectangle. Two circles of different radii determine an oval. Depending on the difference between the large and small radius, the oval will be more or less pointy or round. It is the difference (of course) between the lengths of the radii, which creates the dynamic of the oval form. The egg form is a combination of a sphere and an oval.

THE CIRCLE AND OVAL ARE THE ORGANIC VERSIONS OF THE SQUARE AND THE RECTANGLE. THE DYNAMIC OF THE OVAL COMES FROM THE DIFFERENCE BETWEEN THE LARGE AND SMALL RADIUS.

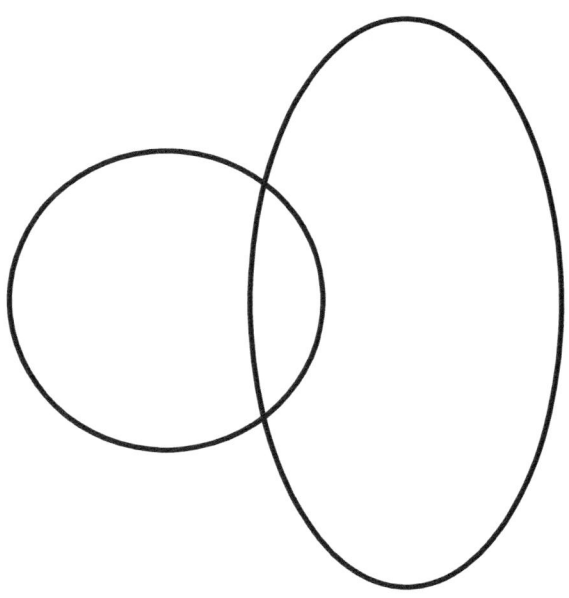

Apartment block Zug. 2007. Arch. V. Olgiati. Photo B.A.J.

The oval above is very dynamic – but on the verge of being pointed in the ends. The difference in expression between the old and new oval is quite astonishing. This one is full of tension and movement. The ability to connect the sight of a curve to an experience of inner tension is crucial for our unique and emotional relationship with curves. If the arch comes close to being straight, this immediately reduces the impression of both tension and movement.

This baroque oval is more static and on the verge of being flat on the sides, in contrast to the previous one in Zug. The difference is even more evident in the central lantern. These lines are much calmer – and suits the purpose of contemplation in the cloister church. Both the new and the old oval have a significant structure and use repetition to emphasize the perspective, whether it is false or real. Contrasting geometric forms create a pattern inside the cupolas.

San Carlo Alle Quattro Fontane. 1641. Arch. F. Borromini. Photo T.A.J

ORGANIC FORM

TYPES OF FORM:

CIRCLE, ELLIPSE, OVAL, EGG-SHAPED, WAVE-FORM, DROP, SNAKE FORM, SPIRAL, AMOEBIC FORM, PARABOLIC AND HYPERBOLIC FORM.

BASIC ELEMENTS: CURVE, SPIRAL, SERPENTINE, S-LINE, CONCAVE, CONVEX.

MOVEMENT: AVAILABLE IN ALL BASIC ELEMENTS.

STILL: CIRCLE, SPHERE.

ORGANIC SHAPES

Staircase on a silo in Aalborg. Photo T.A.J

In this spiral staircase, the number of linear elements exceeds the curved parts. Only the handrail and the edge of the steps curve, but never the less, the thin continuous bar dominates the design and makes the whole structure appear organic. The oblique lines of the rotating straight steps around the spine, support the impression of movement.

CURVED + STRAIGHT

Connecting the circle with the straight line creates a cylinder. The cylindrical form is a hybrid of organic and geometric. Its quality is a simple combination of soft and hard.

The simple opposition between curved and straight represents several related contradictions: movement versus still, active versus passive, expressive versus neutral, involvement versus abstraction.

Therefore, a straight line or a plain surface enables us to "slow-down" or stop the dynamic in curves. The straight line adds a break, a pause, in the movement – and takes away the tension. But looking at this phenomenon from the opposite point of view, the straight line becomes dynamic attached to a curve.

Single curved forms being both rectilinear (in one direction) and curved (in another), like a tube or a cone, have movement in one direction, but not in the other. Depending on what dominates, this pushes the overall perception of the shape towards geometric or organic.

Oblique lines, which already have some "stiff movement", quickly transform this to a much more dynamic movement if combined with curves.

Single-curved surfaces have a significantly less organic expression than double-curved. So a single-curved form has less movement and less tension than a double-curved. We must see and understand these forms as hybrids.

Turning Torso. Malmø 2005. Arch. S. Calatrava Photo T.A.J

The human preference for curves makes us see arches even when they are non-existing. It is possible to make straight lines appear as curves if they are combined wisely. The "Turning Torso" is a study in illusions because the turning twist is a combination of oblique straight lines. The structural arch, the backbone of the building, looks curved but is made of straight-line sections welded together with smooth transitions. The facades of the apartment boxes look curved, but even they are made by straight-lined panels.

This double-curved organic structural design is a hybrid form. Our preference for continuity and curves dominates the perception and "overrule" the patterns of straight lines. The roof is much more dynamic than a single-curved form. The repetitive structure of "squares" under the roof cover, gradually change size, shape and direction. These oblique lines make the geometric rectangles look more dynamic - fitting into an organic unity. Just like the patterns on the opera house, these geometric shapes add an element of rational order and control to the dynamic movement.

Olympic Stadium in Munich 1972. Arch. Frei Otto. Photo T.A.J

Office building near Hackesche Markt, Berlin. Photo T.A.J.

This elegant round glass corner combining straight and curved form demonstrate a contrast of (mirroring) mass and thin structure.
The form is cylindrical and convex and adds a soft organic expression to the otherwise geometric glass building. The protruding sharp and dark horizontal structure is in contrast to the smooth continuous surface of the glossy glass. The contrasting lines emphasize the dynamic of the curves. The passive horizontal line becomes "dynamic" when attached to an arch and supported by the effect of perspective.

The arcade at Parc Guel illustrates how well the oblique straight lines interact with the curve and create motion and dynamic. This famous tilting space is extreme: it conflicts so violently with our sense of balance, that we tend to ignore it is motionless. Mixed structural form to the left, solid organic at top - solid geometric to the right.

Arcade Parc Güel. 1914. Arch. A. Gaudi. Photo T.A.J.

Our Lady Church. Harissa. Lebanon Photo T.A.J

MASS
&
STRUCTURE

WHAT ARE
MASS & STRUCTURE?

It is not possible to regard the opposites Mass and Structure as a type of form, but rather as a condition associated with geometric and organic shape. A form cannot be massive or structural by itself; its shape interacts with the basic types of form. Like other pairs of opposites, Mass and Structure have a long series of gradations in between the extremes. The gradual transformation of a tree, from the massive stem to the branch structure, illustrates the principle. The leaves demonstrate how the plane is a hybrid, looking solid form one side and as a thin structure form the other. The more solid and robust a grid becomes, the more mass-oriented it appears. But in the Circle of Form structure fades away towards the bottom because the volume becomes more and more dominant.
In the extreme Mass becomes a solid without any grid.

Conversely, the more a form appears with thin planes, lines, grids and voids, the more structural will appear. The extreme version of Structure is a void, like the opening in the cupola of Pantheon.

In the Circle of Form, the empty space in a grid or a hole in a solid, the void, is part of the model. Structural form is open and subdivided because the shape is reduced to a grid, whereas the mass-oriented form has a closed surface and a coherent volume. Structural form often requires a more profound knowledge of statics and materials, because the form minimizes into a grid. The impression of Mass and Structure closely relates to what we experience as heaviness and lightness.

Erasmus Bridge. Rotterdam. 1996 Ark. Ben V. Berkel & Bos Ph. T.A.J

The pillar represents volume and mass contrasting the structural bridge deck above. The contrast is easy to read. Where the support and the bridge deck meet is a hidden connection, creating a distance between support and deck, giving the latter an expression of lightness. The shape of the pillar change from organic to geometric, creating a similarity between the beam and the support.

The Circle of Form model does not account for whether something is physically heavy or light, but only if it looks solid, volume-like or structural, grid-like. Yet, we typically perceive a structural form as more light than a bulky one.
On the other hand, it is possible to make a massive form seems light if it spreads upwards or the volume appears to float above without the impression of gravity. If the form/structure opens up and becomes more structural, you will achieve ease and an aspiring effect. The opposite, on the other hand, will have a gravitational effect.

When structure "condenses", becomes voluminous, it shifts from Structure to Mass.

Voluminous for- and backward offsets in a building façade, like the solid base structure used in old buildings, make it look heavier and more massive than if it has smooth surfaces.
Reversing Mass and Structure (the impression of heavy and light) therefore, can achieve exciting expressions. The exterior of Doge's Palace in Venice is a famous example of just such a reverse use; of the heavy volume upon the light grid of pointed arches. The Wozoco building is demonstrating an even more provocative way of the dramatic effect of this.

Wozoco Amsterdam. 1997. Arch. MVRDV. Photo T.A.J

The building above looks quite impossible. The boxes protruding from the facade are the result of a need for 13 extra apartments added to the project. The solution was radical, both constructively, architecturally. The apartments were hung on the external surface. Not only do the apartment boxes protrude provocatively. They are challenging our sense of balance and gravity.

While the concrete building carrying them, has a light and fragile glass façade, the design of the apartment boxes are "massive" and appear heavy. This creates a dramatic expression employing contrasts between heavy and light, mass and structure.

Pantheon in Rome. Photo: T.A.J.

The Pantheon cupola has a fascinating composition of contrasting organic and geometric forms. The overall shape of the vault is organic while the structure inside is geometric - but slightly curved. The circular oculus at the top represents the ultimate contrast to the massive vault.

The solid trapeze-shaped structure, with a stepped bas relief that emphasises the geometric form, contrasts the curved vault. The patterns are stepwise reduced in size and then at the top replaced by a large plain circular surface: A neutral frame before the contrasting opening to the sky.

Top tower. Almere. Netherlands. Photo T.A.J

In this cubical form with a mass-oriented, geometric structure, the repetition of the deep relief in the facade creates a significantly powerful expression. When a building facade become 3-dimensional, the appearance becomes more expressive because it interacts with the surrounding space. The monotony of the façade motif highlights the "randomly" placed large square windows. Repetitions are an ideal background for these simple variations. The corners are projecting into the air without support. They open the cubic structure and create the impression of a double cube: a fragile glass volume covered with a massive concrete grid.

Sankt Benedikt Chapel. 1989. Arch. P. Zumthor Photo: B.A.J.

Solid curved form with a rough horizontal geometric texture on the surface dominates the walls on the outside, while a slim vertical structure with windows dominates the top.

The contrast is significant, but the similarity of materials maintain the overall impression of unity. As an opposition to the exterior, a variety of slim grids and smooth surfaces dominate the interior. This exterior-interior contrast is the opposite of his later Bruder Klaus Kapelle.(p.128)

PATTERN & TEXTURE

When scaling down and looking at the phenomenon of Mass and Structure in relation to surfaces, it is called pattern and texture. The expression of surfaces follows some of the same principles, known from the larger scale. However, the Circle of Form is not a model developed for describing surfaces, patterns and textures even though many of the phenomenon's fits into the four contrasting categories. Perhaps if we perceive the surface as an extra layer of form added to the object, this helps the understanding.

Patterns with sharp lines introduce the phenomenon of Structure to a volume, like a net put on top of the form. The lines are easy to read. They will often dominate; therefore, it is possible to tighten a blobby form up with a geometric pattern or ad some organic movement to a static form with undulating lines. The phenomenon is somehow similar to the effect of combining organic and geometric form – but more subtly. Patterns of colour can do the same thing.
The examples show how this affects perception and expression.

Texture adds to our experience of the material. A rough surface makes the object "physical" or "tactile". A crystalline surface is more "hard" and geometric, while a smooth surface is more "soft" when we touch it – but also hard and cold if the material has that character. Once again, we find a system of opposites defining the differences: glossy or mat, soft or hard, smooth or rough, rounded or sticky.

Olivetti showroom. 1958 Venezia. Arch. Carlo Scarpa. Photo: B.A.J.

Olivetti showroom. 1958 Venezia. Arch. Carlo Scarpa. Photo: B.A.J.

In small scale, Mass and Structure express itself through texture and pattern. Carlo Scarpa was a master in both of these disciplines and often used them as contrasts: Plane, smooth versus crystalline coarse, warm golden brass versus cold grey stone.

The unique craftsmanship emphasizes these contrasting details. The elegant and expressive combination of Istrian stone and a geometric design in brass, placed where three straight lines and the stone panels intersect.

The relief above shows the contrast between another type of texture of the Istrian stone and the precise line of smoothly carved letters - the difference between organic coarse and smooth works perfectly.

The slightly curved frontal surface of the letters makes them look even more "soft". As opposition to this, the sharp, thin and straight horizontal lines in the letters contrast the otherwise "chubby" character. A smooth surface is very neutral. The context, the form, determine whether it is perceived geometric or organic.

Brick wall. Amsterdam. Photo T.A.J

The wall above has a repetitive geometric pattern - but the variations in the colour display a subtle floating organic movement.

The straight geometric surface restricts the impression of movement. This double perception of organic and geometric adds to the aesthetic quality - compared to a wall with identical monotonous stones. Yet, in the Circle of Form, colours are not part of the model, but in many aspects, their patterns act just like form.

The woven panels form a series of "standing waves", or S-lines. The protruding geometric framings of the doors are contrasting the wall's organic movement. They introduce a static, repetitive element of control, to this overwhelming impression of movement.

The woven surface - made of thick round iron "thread" - is undulating like the facade, but the horizontal and vertical lines add a structural geometric pattern to the undulating form.

Compared to the brick wall, it is somehow the same - but the other way around. The modular assembly lines dominate the wall, thus reducing the visual effect of organic unity.

St. Guy's hospital. 2007. Arch. Thomas Heatherwick. Photo B.A.J

So, in patterns, lines, coarse and sticky surfaces we see a reference to Structure in both geometric and organic form.

Crystalline, rough surfaces with straight-lined facets, refers to Geometric Mass.

Undulating uneven surfaces with concave and convex forms refers to Organic Mass.

An even surface is neutral - just like the smooth solid volume at the bottom of the Circle of form.

When the surface of an otherwise massive form becomes glossy and reflecting, it loses a lot of its solid appearance, because the surface does the opposite. It becomes transparent. Like glass with mullions being solid, but often in an analysis of form and contrast, will be regarded as grid and void – because it is transparent.

MASS & STRUCTURE

MASS EMBODIES SURFACE AND VOLUME. STRUCTURE EMBODIES LINE, GRID AND VOID.

MASS AND STRUCTURE ARE NOT A TYPE OF FORM, BUT A STATE WHICH GEOMETRIC AND ORGANIC FORM CAN HAVE.

MASS AND STRUCTURE OFTEN REFER TO THE EXPERIENCE OF HEAVINESS AND LIGHTNESS.

IN SMALL SCALE, MASS AND STRUCTURE DEFINE QUALITIES OF THE SURFACE: TEXTURE AND PATTERN.

GRID & VOLUME

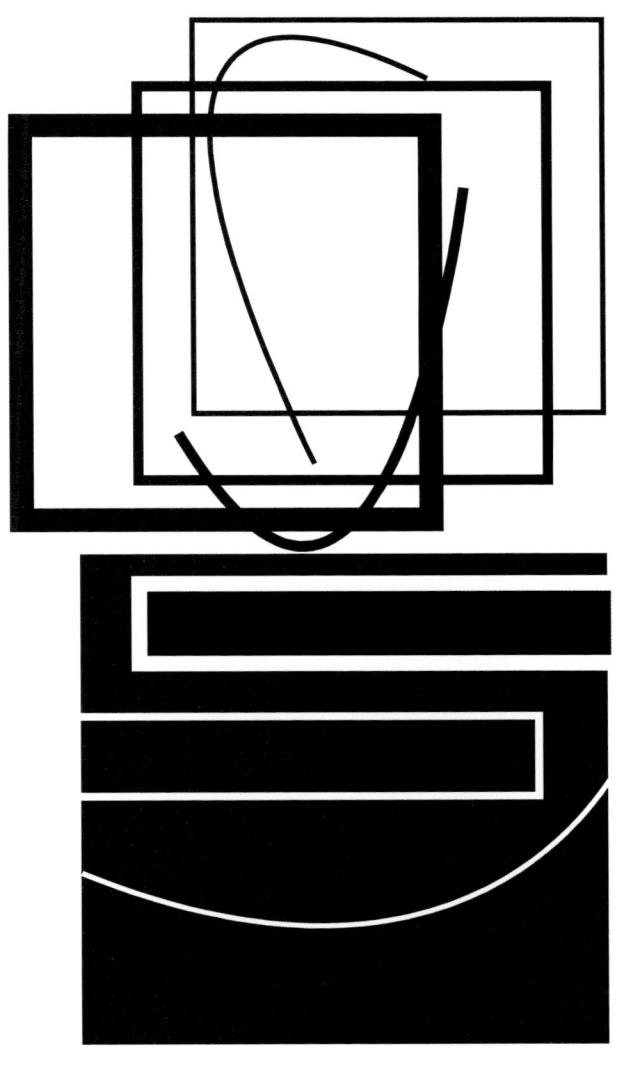

Chest of drawers. 1991. Droog Design Tejo Remy. Photo T.A.J

SEPARATE OR UNITE?

TRANSITION AND MEETING

TRANSITION & MEETING

The previous chapters have focused on the different types of form, but a closer look at how they encounter is necessary because the meeting "articulates" the dialogue between the forms. Architecture rarely consists of just a single form or a single material. Often, multiple elements, parts and materials are present, and they must relate to each other individually and to the whole.
Here, the Circle of Form, with its rules about contrasts and harmonies becomes relevant.

Besides, the choices of form and composition, transitions and meetings are necessary elements supporting the narrative understanding of how the various parts relate to each other. The way forms encounter, tell us about how we should understand the shapes themselves and their relationships. Every time two surfaces or materials meet, there is a choice to be made.

There is a wide range of concepts for the different types of meetings or junctions: forms can slip into each other, overlap, connect, integrate or clash. A meeting can be marked by a protrusion or a concave void, lying in shadow or otherwise hidden. Edges, markings, shifts in surfaces or materials are important instruments in the language of form, as they split the surface, create lines, form differences.

British Museum. Arch. Foster & Partners. Photo: B.A.J.

Two types of transitions between the glass structural glass roof and a contrasting building: The classic building to the right looks at it has a protruding stepwise transition from wall to the glazing structure above, even though the actual junction between the roof and the wall is a clash, hidden above the corniche.

The modern building has a simplified version of the same motive designed as a protruding ribbon with inscriptions and a dark ring with a row of lighting fixtures. This meeting represents an integration with the contrasting roof and creates an impression of unity.

STEPWISE TRANSITION: FROM ORGANIC COLUMN TO GEOMETRIC BASE

A smooth organic transition from vertical to horizontal.

Semi geometric form stops the movement.

Small convex form - a prelude to the huge compressed convex form below (contrast in scale but similarity in form).

Shift from organic to geometric shape marked by shaded void.

Contrasting geometric cubic form. A prelude for the horizontal plane and tiles.

Sct. Peter. Roman doric order. Arch. Bernini 1656-67. Photo T.A.J

STEPWISE TRANSITION: FROM SEMI-ORGANIC CURVED RIBS TO GEOMETRIC/CRYSTALLINE AND ORGANIC BASE

A row of stepped forms changes the dynamic curved ribs to straight-lined crystaline, geometric form.

Geometric flat straight ribs – a neutral form stretching out between the dramatic opposites.

A conical void under a protuding form – a prelude to the crystalline forms above and contrasting the smooth curved form below.

Compressed convex organic solid unite the multiple geometric structures above.

A recess/void as a prelude to the protruding convex form above. A straight surface meets the floor

Sydney Opera. Base of shell. Arch. J. Utzon. 1957- Photo T.A.J

The term stepwise refers to the design of a staircase. Whether it is straight or curved, it influences the way we experience the spaces it connects. Descending into a room is something quite different from ascending. It changes the way we experience the space.

The character of the previous primes our perception of the present.

Details in the meeting between different forms tell us how to understand the composition: If the overall expression has a decisive weight on the homogeneous, the differences between the various parts must be minimized, and transitions should support this concept. If a composition focuses on a dialogue between different parts, these must appear clearly, and their relations must focus on significant divisions, diversity and contrasts.

Aarhus City Hall. Arch. A. Jacobsen 1944. Photo T.A.J

The curved staircase creates a stepwise connection between cellar and ground floor in Arne Jacobsen's City Hall.
The sweeping curve is contrasting the straight steps and the geometric floor pattern.
Stepwise is also a term used to describe for transitions between the forms in a composition.

SEPARATE

Herzberger's theatre in Breda illustrates an overall concept of dividing a composition into distinctive parts: The dark scene tower and the white audience wall under the curved rooftop stand apart from the roofs above and below. The diagonal staircases make a distinctive projection on the facade and the corner pillar projects from the building to carry the roof, which does not follow the building below. The sloping roof comes down to the white wall, without touching it.

Between the old brick house and the new building, the meeting expresses a respectful distance with a transparent glass section, but otherwise, this meeting is a dramatic clash. The language of form is about "non-unification".

Herzberger prefers differences and contrasts. Every element tells its own story about what it is doing. All the meetings follow this concept with great consistency and show how difficult it is has been to execute.

The curved roofs, white concrete walls and glass facades do create a sense of unity in this complex composition. The theatre plays with all four elements of the Circle of Form: mass and structure, straight and curved form.

Rear facades of the Chasse Theatre. Breda. Arch. Herman Hertzberger 1995. Photo T.A.J

101

UNITE

Mendelsohn's Einsteinturm illustrates the opposite strategy of Hertzberger's. How a composition with four very different parts effortlessly fuses into a unity, when the overall concept is organic.

The four different parts are the staircase/terrace, the entrance hall, the tower and the offices to the rear. The smooth plaster surface on the facades contributes to the overall effect of organic unity. A closer look on the building discloses many oppositions: geometric straight lines and surfaces combining straight and curved – so the architecture is a mix, a hybrid, but with emphasis on the curve.

The fifth part of the building, the cellar/basement, participates in the composition as an opposition: a flat geometric grassy podium in contrast to the organic architecture rising above it. When looking at transitions in the facade, surfaces slide over each other and merge the shapes, while deep cuts create a massive structure, making openings for the windows and their contrasting geometric frame structure. On the backside of the tower, the middle surface leaps forward and creates a prelude to the recessed round window shutter. Where the concave surfaces meet, they form sharp, expressive edges. At the entrance, the oblique straight cut of the staircase changes the whole expression dramatically: from just being a staircase to a piece of crystalline sculpture. Notice the delicate transitions.

Einsteinturm Potsdam 1919. Arch. E. Mendelsohn. Photo B.A.J

103

Fondazione Prada. Milano. 2015 OMA Architects. Photo:BAJ.

An excellent strategy for solving complex meetings between very different types of form is to keep a distance.

A controlled clash between opposites: the modern and the old building meet each other dramatically. The closed facade opens with a sharp angular cut so, the structure becomes visible before the new and the old building meet each other: interacting but without touching each other. The void between the two buildings makes this otherwise tricky detail possible.

Dudok's city hall is a symphony of vertical and horizontal, mass and structure.

This part of the exterior wall demonstrates how simple interacting rectangular forms create a massive structure with a variety of contrasting elements.

Volumes, voids, windows and thin projecting slaps create a play of light and shadow. The cubic elements interact in stepwise, hidden, merging and abrupt transitions. The yellow bricks unite the composition.

Town Hall Hilversum. 1924-31. Arch. M. Dudok. Photo T.A.J.

Stilwerk Brücke. Fischmarkt. Hamburg. Arch. Unknown. Photo T.A.J

Kronprinzen Brücke. Berlin 1996. Arch. S. Calatrava. Photo T.A.J

Sliding transition between opposites:
Geometric mass with a thin contrasting structure versus semi-solid organic structure.

The dynamic curve stretches out between the horizontal geometric walkway and the oblique linear pillars. The organic shape at the top of the pillars is a decorative sheet of iron plate, attached to the geometric post behind. The oblique straight lines of the pillars match the dynamic of the curve and connect to their opposition, the geometric bridge on the top. This upper part of the bridge is static with emphasis on structure and repetition. The sliding transition changes the overall expression from geometric to organic.

Abrupt and stepwise transitions:
Geometric structure versus organic structure.

The loadbearing oblique anchor is geometric, but the curves in the details change the overall expression from sharp geometric (near the base) towards soft organic, matching the design of the bridge. The transition seems abrupt, concentrated in a single hinge. On a closer look, we see how the top of the anchor transforms into a cylinder and a hemisphere, meeting the cylindrical rods, so the transition from anchor to bridge is both sliding and in steps. The meeting between the anchor and the horizontal concrete base is abrupt.

MEETING

MEETINGS AND TRANSITIONS IN FORM REPRESENT OPPOSITIONS:

DIFFERENCE – SIMILARITY

WHOLE – PART

EITHER – OR

MORE – LESS

TRANSITION

PROJECTED OR MARKED TRANSITION: PROTRUDING EDGE, PROTRUDING FORM

HIDDEN TRANSITION: VOID, RECESS, CAVITY

STEPWISE TRANSITION: CHANGING ONE FORM PARAMETER, REPEATING OTHERS – IN STEPS

SLIDING OR MERGING TRANSITION: FORM FADES OUT, FORMS MERGE OR BLEND INTO EACH OTHER

ABRUPT TRANSITION: SUDDEN CHANGE OF FORM, CLASH BETWEEN FORMS

Kunsthaus Bregenz. 1997. Arch. P. Zumthor. Photo. by J.

ANALYZING
FORM AND CONTRASTS

GETTING
A CLEAR PICTURE

In a creative process of design, one must realise: what are the elements in the game? Many questions arise, and typically they will deal with some of the following problems:

What is the central "theme" in the composition in relation to form? Similarity, differences, uniform, split-up, separated.

Which type of form? Straight, curved, a mix of both

How do they appear? Mass, structure

How do these interact? Harmonic similarity, diversity, contrast.

Which kind of form dominate and subordinate? Scale differences and hierarchy.

What other types of opposites do we find: still or movement, inside or outside, variation or repetitions, symmetry or asymmetry etc.?

What kind of transitions are used and how do they support the general theme in the composition?

If the result is going to be successful, these factors need a steady hand during the design process. Related or similar forms create unity, but with too much similarity, the composition risks becoming indifferent or just empty repetitions. Differences, on the other hand, create variation and even drama, but too many different elements create complexity. Forms can enrich or spoil each other. In the design process, the artistic ideas must determine how the individual differences can be part of the whole. Working with opposites, therefore, include a job with adjusting different grades of similarities and differences. Contrast effects can unfold rather subtle: when something looks straight, but curves, when a slight asymmetry plays into a symmetrical composition or a monotonous repetition is made vivid by discrete differences. Contrasts are not a shortcut to great art, but they are an essential part of the language we use to articulate form. Often, contrasts are just reduced to visual provocations because they instantly catch our attention. If not contrasts are well-chosen, play together and are used with artistic sensitivity, they tend to dominate and destroy the overall impact. If they are missing compositions often become rather tedious.

The different analyses this chapter, following the principles of the Circle of Form, describe both similar and contrasting forms and their interactions. The small mapping model at the top corner of each analysis offers a simplified interpretation of the composition. Is was developed for teaching purposes, to shortcut long written descriptions of form and design. They tend to be long and difficult conclude on - but of course have other qualities in order to create insigt.
On the other hand, understanding the nature of a specific design is about making things simple and straightforward. Getting a clear picture. So the examples in this last chapter use both methods. The mapping model is, of course, neither very precise nor able to include all aspects of a piece of work, but it can map the most significant parts of a building and their relations. The process of mapping demands some "slow thinking", just like a written description, but afterwards, the result is much faster to read.
(Description of method in Appendix 1).

FRANK GEHRY
GEOMETRIC AND ORGANIC
MASS AND STRUCTURE

The main motive of this composition is the contrast between the geometric wood-panel structure, surrounding the entire internal courtyard and the organic, sculptural meeting space covered with shiny metal. This large, undulating form is situated directly between two other contrasting forms: a transparent glass roof-grid and a crystalline light-reflecting glass "floor" – a roof covering the space below.
The geometric-structural walls have a warm, reddish-brown wood, sharp-edged and orthogonal. The contrasting meeting space in the middle has a shell-like continuous solid organic form. The exterior coated with shining silver metal looks cold and hard, but with warm reddish wood inside. The form is asymmetrical, in contrast to its symmetrical repetitive surroundings.
A crystalline convex volume form beneath represents similarity and a contrast to the roof and the organic meeting room. Solid instead of structural, geometric instead of organic. The expression in this daylight is hard and cold, but in other situations, it will become a transparent grid-like the roof.
Above the courtyard, the roof is a curve-dominated hybrid form. Small, straight grid rods combined into curve-like shapes. The lines create a similarity to the organic meeting room in shape – but with a mass-structure contrast. The use of diagonal "curves" creates extra movement. Transitions: The orthogonal geometric structure along the periphery and the organic volume in the centre do not meet; they are detached. Visually they clash. The glass roof has a 2-step transition to the wooden wall.

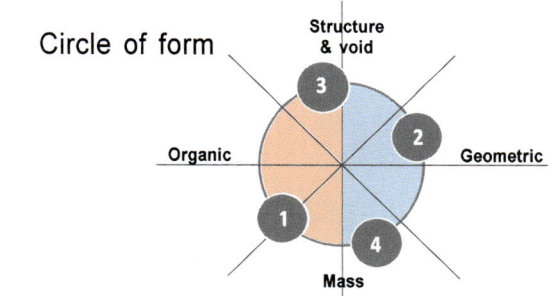

Interior court. DZ Bank. 1999 Berlin. Arch. Frank Gehry. Photo T.A.J

M. FUKSAS
GEOMETRIC CUBIC MASS AND CRYSTALLINE STRUCTURE

The church consists of two cubic boxes, one inside the other. The exterior of the church building is a static closed, grey cube. Inside, the interior white cube hangs from the ceiling, so the cube touches neither the outer walls nor the floor. The inner cube stops approximately three meters from the floor and the outer walls.

A crystalline structure of window "tubes" on the sides connect the inner and outer cube. The sidewalls of the cubes have "randomly" placed, oblique, window tubes, directing light from the outside walls to the interior church nave. These tubes make the thin interior wall look thick and solid. The interior has crystalline shaped lamps hanging from above somehow akin to the form of the windows perforating the walls – but opposites.

The three meters wide but tall narrow space between the outer and inner cube is a walking area, side aisles, around the church nave. Upwards this narrow space is intersected by the oblique angled forms, which gives a surprisingly chaotic, structural, narrow and expressive space in contrast to the calm exterior and interior, both simple and orthogonal.

The square in front of the entrance extends into the closed box, separated only by a broad low horizontal section of glass in the same width as the facade. The church exterior seems closed but also opens toward the square.

The contrast effects used can be described as cubical vs crystalline, simple vs complex, solid vs void, mass vs structure, static vs dynamic, open vs closed, grounded vs floating, high vs low.

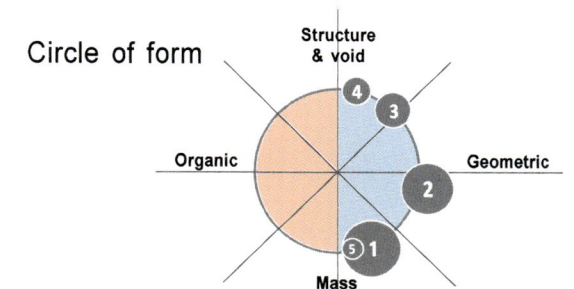

Circle of form

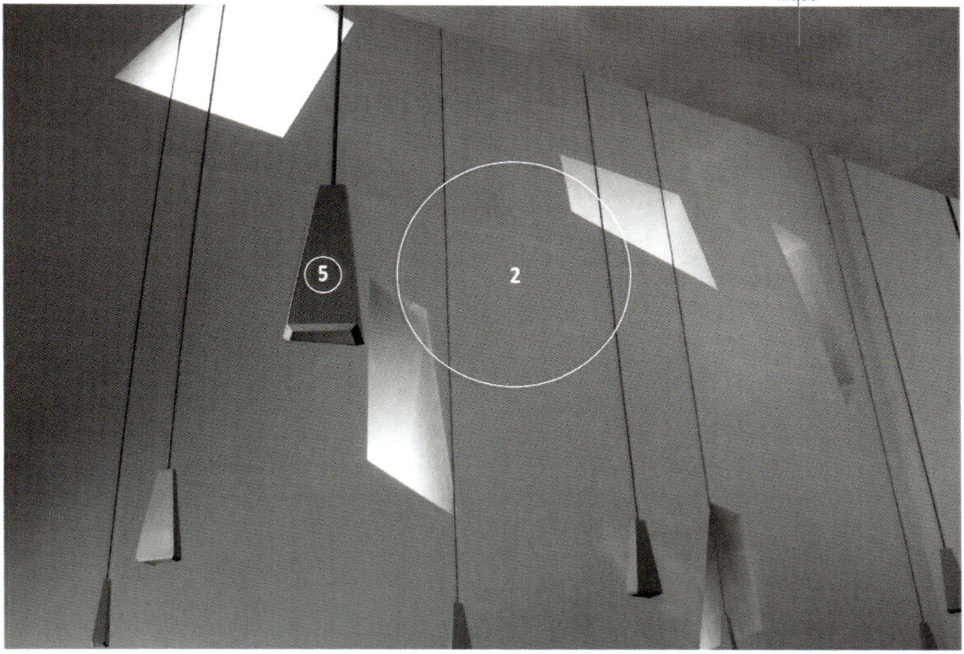

Structure & void
Organic
Geometric
Mass
4
3
2
5
1

5
2

3

1
4

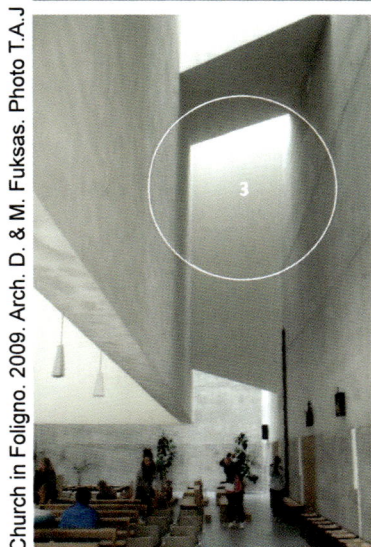

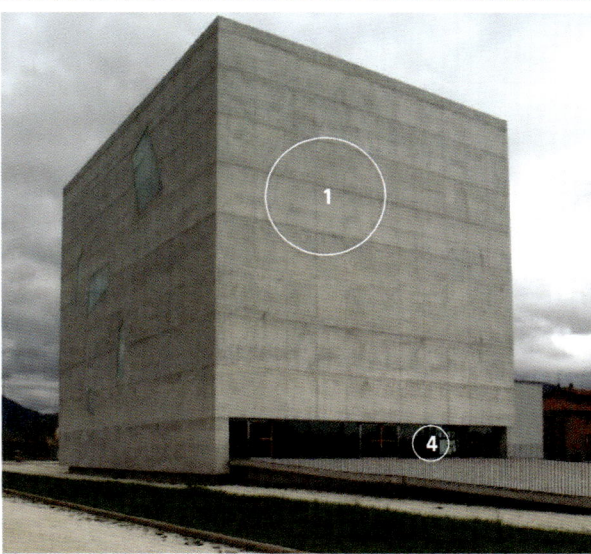

Church in Foligno. 2009. Arch. D. & M. Fuksas. Photo T.A.J

RENZO PIANO
ORGANIC VOLUME AND SOLID GEOMETRIC STRUCTURE

The Auditorium complex consists of three organic-shaped "cupolas" with a geometric structured access area downstairs, located on three sides around an outdoor auditorium space. A rectangular pattern on the organic shapes and a straight horizontal edge below create a similarity, a link, between the organic and the geometric form. Just as the exterior theatre, the music halls are in opposition to the curved shells. The music halls have straight-lined geometric, crystalline walls barely visible under the cupolas. The organic form "hovers" above the amphitheatre. Organic and geometric form are not mixed.

The transition hides in the shadows of a void below the cupolas. However, the patterns of the organic shells are geometric. The straight edges the cupolas play along with the horizontal lines of the geometric forms below.

The open-air theatre below the cupolas is geometric with a robust, mass-oriented structure. Light, sleek travertine plates cover the seats emphasizing the horizontal lines and the contrast to the dark, rough brickwork.

The solid theatre does not meet the courtyard. Just like the cupolas, it hangs above a dark void with glass doors to the foyer area.

The theatre forms a stepped geometric, concave space – creating a dramatic contrast to the convex forms above. The three organic domes dominate upwards, while the extensive geometric form organizes the unity of the building horizontally.

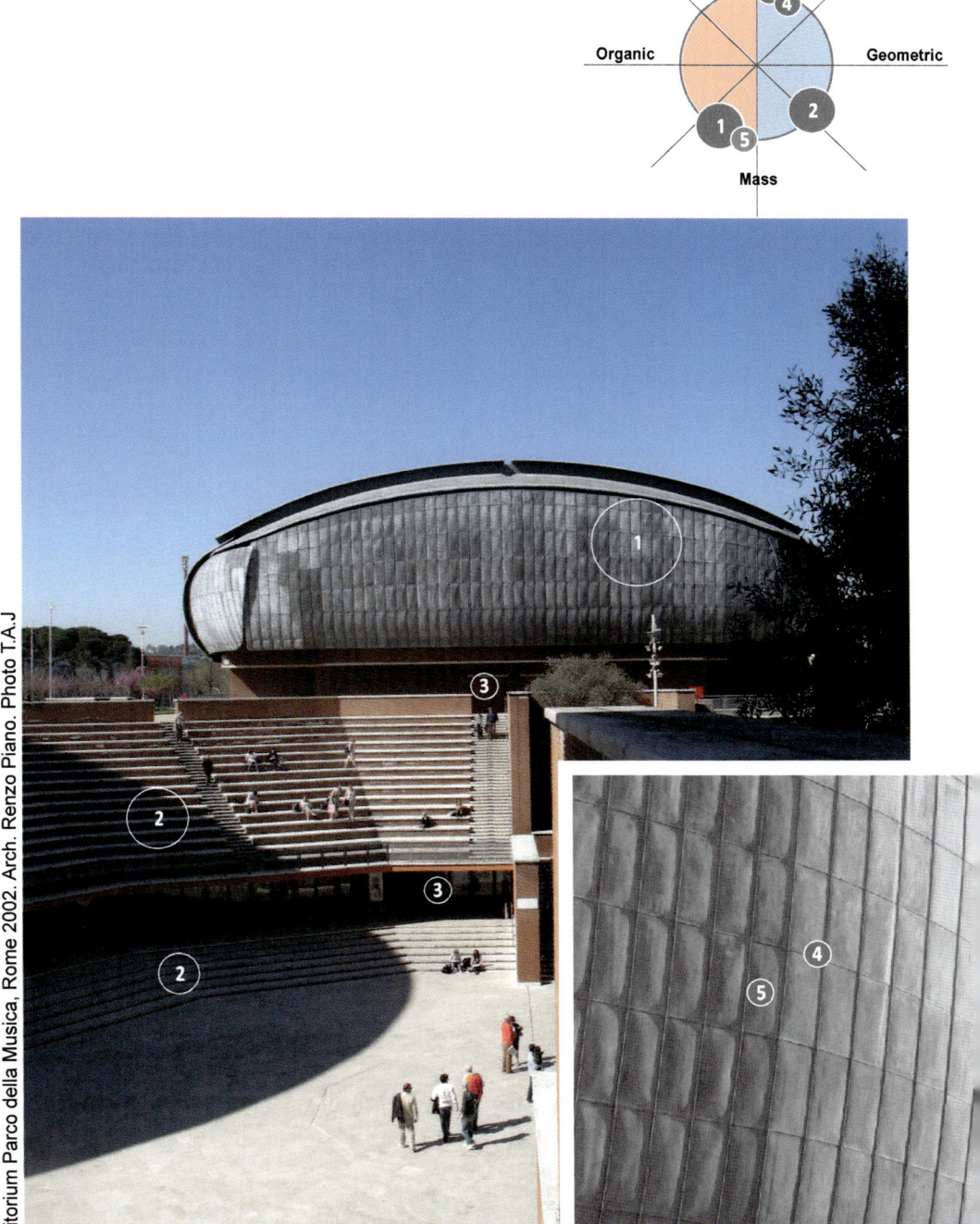

W.GROPIUS & A.MEYER
GEOMETRIC FORM
MASS AND STRUCTURE

The entrance stands in stark contrast to the structural factory building. This section is classical, massive, stands stable on the ground, and completely symmetrical. However, placed asymmetrically in relation to the modern transparent factory in glass and steel. A modern concrete staircase is hanging free, asymmetrical, behind the transparent corner. The classic staircase is symmetric and solid grounded. The entrance has horizontal lines in the brickwork, while the factory building's window sections are vertical – but with a thin grid of mullions matching the horizontal module. The windows hang outside the brick façade, but level with the brick cornice above them – otherwise, the meeting between iron, glass and brick is abrupt and do not merge. The solid door is retracted but with modern rounded corners. There is a peculiar detail. The narrow piece of façade between the windows, the recess, is not vertical. It tilts slightly inwards in the vertical direction, resulting in a more significant relief at the top cornice. This detail thus adds a discrete complexity and gravity of the wall. Yellow brick is the recurring material binding the whole building together including the modern architrave above the windows. The horizontal lines and strips of blind windows match the brickwork recesses. Looking at the transitions between the elements and the architecture in a broader perspective the façade tells a story of two eras clashing: a solid, heavy traditional classicism with symmetry versus the light structural modern functionalism with asymmetry. The tilting walls add a hint to something beyond the pure rational logic.

VALERIO OLGIATI
GEOMETRIC AND ORGANIC
OPEN VOID AND SOLID CLOSED

The house has several contradictions, the most significant being a closed external geometric volume, with a space inside, open to the sky through a circular cut in the ceiling. The exterior has only one rectangular opening, to a large open courtyard, next to a music studio. The entrance staircase has a slightly oblique angle as an invitation to access the buildings otherwise totally closed facade. However, when entering the house, the visitor is actually stepping out into its open-air courtyard, dominated by the vast circular cut in the ceiling.

Opposites: Solid exterior geometric volume vs the open and semi-organic interior court structure. Circular open ceiling vs the overall straight-lined walls. The walls emphasize the rectangular cut for a balcony – with a sliding door making it possible to close the building's exterior. When open, it allows a stunning view into the courtyard and upwards through the house and roof to the old houses above. Simple geometric vs decorated organic: randomly placed stylized pattern with flowers in contrast to the simple and tightly composed body of the building. Simplicity vs complexity in comparison to the architecture of the village: smooth cast and simplified modern concrete construction volume without eaves in contrast to the surrounding traditional wooden houses with large eaves, protruding beams, decorations and a wealth of details.

Unity between new and old: form, volume and scale of the new building repeat its surroundings. The new house has a local symbol, a stylized flower, all over the walls – old houses have natural ones below the windows.

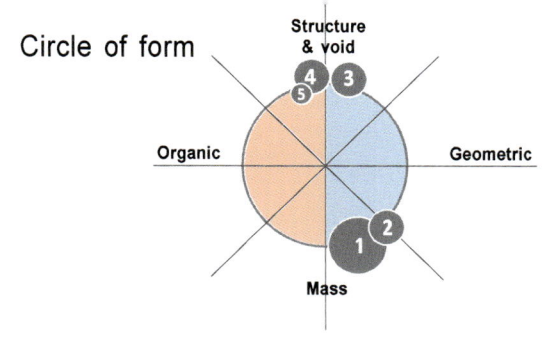

Circle of form

Music Studio in Scharans, Switzerland, Arch. V. Olgiati. Photo: B.A.J.

LE CORBUSIER
CONCAVE AND CONVEX
STRAIGHT AND CURVED

The dominant contrast, as seen from the South-East is the dark grey, sweeping, smooth roof versus the white rough-washed walls.

The concrete roof is convex and pushes the interior space of the chapel downwards. In contrast to this, the dark roof rests on a horizontal void of glass on top of the wall. The heavy ceiling becomes floating. Direct side lights enter the nave through small cuts in the solid wall towards the South and emphasize the horizontal while a deep vertical cut with a concrete structure towards east open the building in this direction.

In contrast to the curved walls and rounded towers, the sloping south-facing facade forms a sharp, sticky, straight-lined corner. The vertical wall supporting the large roof implies symmetry: geometric niches left vs geometric objects right, a tower to the left mirrors roof support to the right. The protruding roof, the tower and perforated walls form a complex, concave space outside the church to the South and East (in opposition to the North and West facades not shown).

The plan is entirely organic with concave and convex lines. The only exception is the straight wall on the steep south-facing wall with deep withdrawn windows. In the vertical direction, on the other hand, the straight dominates with a simple logic: when the wall curves it is vertical, where the wall is straight, it tilts inward. The vertical makes the dynamic curves static, and the oblique makes the straight dynamic. This church has many other motives and interpretations, which go beyond this type of analysis.

Circle of form

PLAN

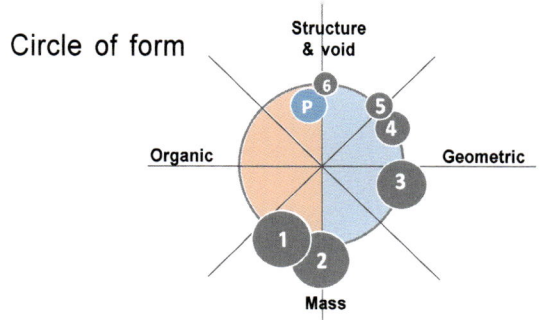

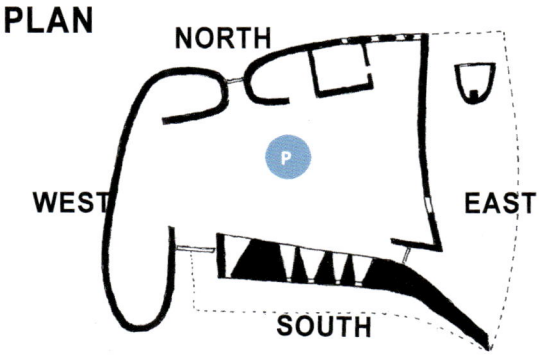

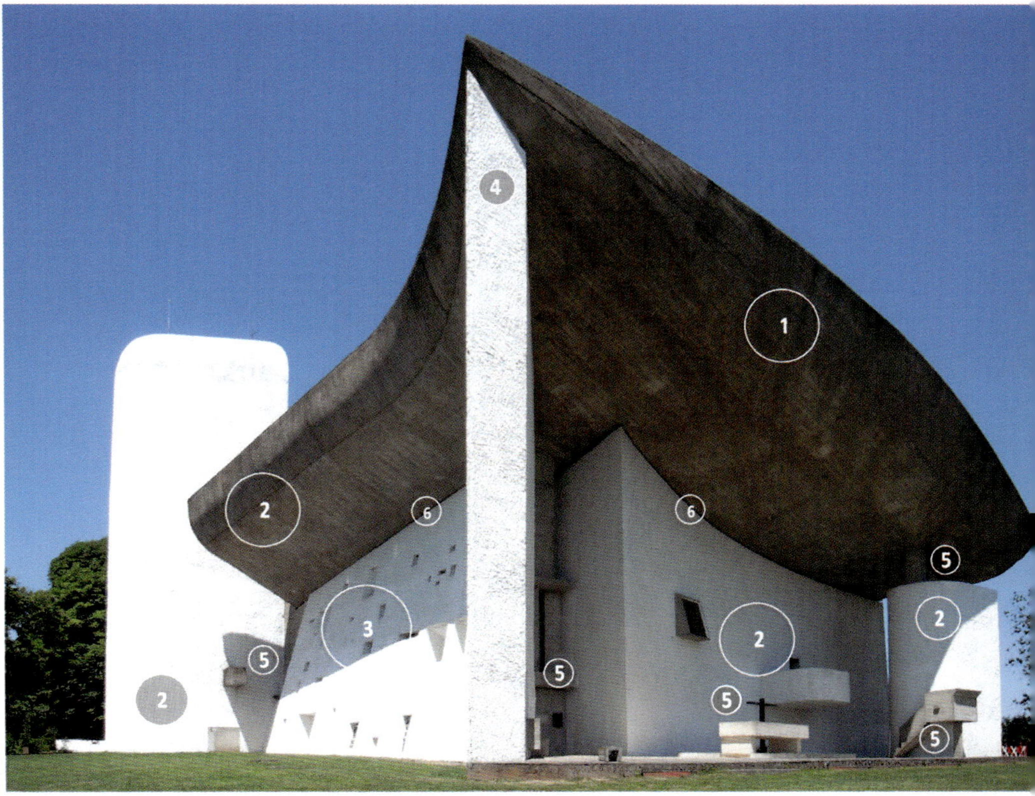

Notre Dame du Haut 1955. Arch. Le Corbusier. Photo: B.A.J.

PETER EISENMAN
GEOMETRIC MASS AND STRUCTURE
VERTICAL AND SLIGHTLY OBLIQUE

A "park" filled with square grey concrete blocks in straight rows, may seem like a paradox as a motive for a Holocaust Memorial, which commemorates human sufferings. Cubic form with sharp edges supports the expression of being cold and hard. Round edges would destroy this. The Memorial uses the repetitive geometric form as a method to highlight the contradictions of the composition and set focus on variation and complexity.

The single parts are solid cubes with sharp edges, while the whole Memorial is like a mass dominated structure. Dislocations and height differences create an experience of the stiff movement in the motionless geometric landscape made by stepped blocks. Slight imbalances in relation to vertical, as well as height differences, do the same: slightly changing the uniform and motionless in the direction of being unique and vivid. The small variations make this extremely simple looking geometrical composition astonishing complex. The recurrence, the monotony, is a tool exploited to emphasize the small differences.

The orthogonal system creates footpaths between the rows. The terrain slopes and change the path from being low and easy to navigate among to a vertical labyrinthine, hard, cold and claustrophobic space. Think about how a soft rounded edge on cubes would destroy this impression. The Memorial plays skillfully on these ambiguities between form and expression.

The many other historical and metaphorical interpretations of the Memorial go beyond the scope of this form analysis.

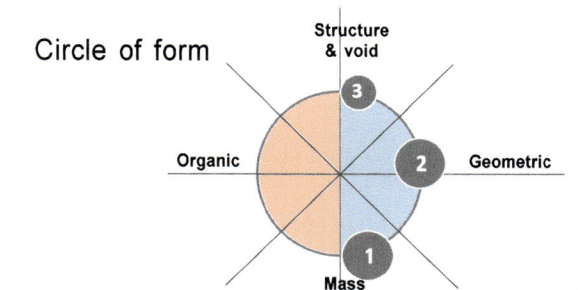

Circle of form

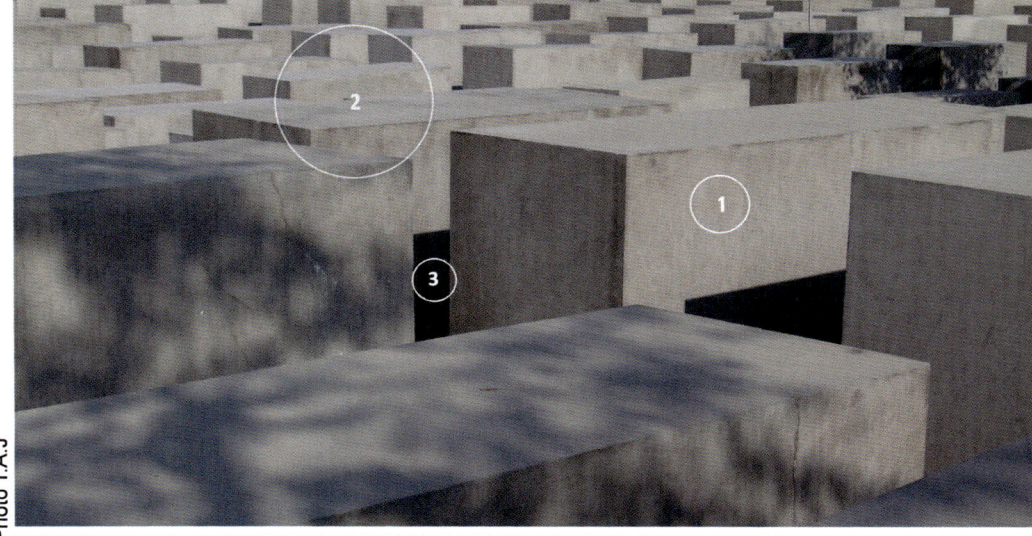

Memorial to the murdered Jews of Europe, Berlin 2005. Arch. Peter Eisenman. Photo T.A.J

127

PETER ZUMTHOR
GEOMETRIC AND ORGANIC
LIGHT AND DARK, SMOOTH AND COARSE

The modest geometric chapel in the field provides a simple vertical contrast to the undulating horizonthal landscape. The building itself is filled with contradictions - even in the way it was built.

The chapel walls, constructed with stamped concrete around a formwork of wooden poles, form an amoeba-like organic interior plan. The walls raise into a conical tent shape with an opening at the top. When the concrete work was finished, its interior was set on fire!

During a period of 3 weeks, the inner wooden formwork slowly burned and left the walls with rough straight-lined ribs, dark and burned.

The contrast between the simple precise geometric exterior - with an organic touch, created by undulating layers of gray-brown concrete - and the rough curved organic dark interior cave with a geometric straight-lined touch from the wooden poles, is the central theme of Zumpthor's design. Spheres of glass inserted into metal tubes perforating the walls, shine like stars in the dark.

The interior is open in the top. The triangular steel door contrasts with the facade but tells something about the shape of the hallway you enter.

The floor is a an alloy of tin and lead, melted and poured out, creating an uneven organic floating texture, referring to the organic pattern on the walls outside and the rough interior. The chapel demonstrates a consequent use of contrasts and similarities, from concept to detail.

APPENDIX 1
METHOD OF ANALYSIS

It is necessary to split the composition into different parts in order to define the form of each part Each icon represents one or more similar forms. The model reflects this division using numbered icons. Their position tells if they are alike, different or oppositions. The size of the icon reflects size in the composition from the view(s) analysed. In simple compositions characterised by similarity, the number of icons will be few and typically only placed in one or two quadrants. In a complex composition, the number of icons often increase and will often be distributed in all quadrants. When a composition consists of hybrid forms, like a cylinder, place the icon in the middle area around the vertical axis. If straight dominates curved form in the view analysed, place the icon with its central part in the geometric area and the minor in the curved and vice versa.

Along the vertical axis, place the icons defining forms dominated by structure/void in the top area. In architecture, windows with mullions typical belong up here unless they are reflecting light and becomes solid-like. In compositions where void/openings are important as contrast to the solid – these voids belongs to the top of the model. Icons defining forms dominated by mass and continuous surfaces belong in the bottom area. If the form has a solid structure with offsets, like a concrete staircase, the icon referring to this belongs around the diagonal line. At the bottom of the circle, icons are representing a simple geometric/organic volume without structure. When a composition is a hybrid between mass and structure place the icon around the horizontal axis.

CIRCLE OF FORM
METHOD OF ANALYSIS

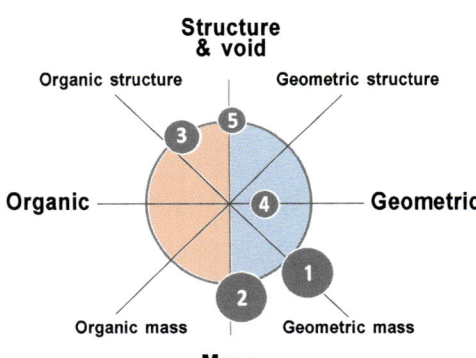

Numbers are random - posistion and size refers to the specific types of form on the building analysed.

① Geometric form. Mass with solid structure. Major size part.

② Mixed solid form, geometric form dominate organic. Major part.

③ Organic form. Thin structure - voids dominate. Medium part.

④ Geometric form - with minor curves. Mass and structure. Minor part.

⑤ Mixed form. Geometric equals organic, thin structure or transparent void. Minor part.

Icons placed above the horizontal axis define forms with structure and void. Below the line, forms become solid and massive. Of course, voids can appear in this part, not as a structure but rather as a minor contrast to solid surface-dominated form.

The model has some limitations: it does not tell something about the "internal" oppositions in geometric (vertical/horizontal/oblique) and organic (concave/convex) form.

Personal opinion is, of course, involved in many of the decisions, not our taste, but rather our ability to define form. Either-or definitions of forms near the poles are easy. It is the more-less decisions that are troublesome – but when doubt about form enters, reflection begins, and the Circle of Form sets up a *simple frame* for discussions. Furthermore, some types of form are not easy to describe just with one position of an icon, but by spitting the form and using two icons instead of one can be a solution.

.

REFERENCES

Arnheim, Rudolf. 1977. The dynamics of Architectual form. University of California Press Ltd. London.

Arnheim, Rudolf. 1954/74. Visual Perception: A Psychology of the Creative Eye. University of Californa Press.

Arvid Jaeger, Thomas. 2019. Modsætninger:
Teorier om form og kontraster. (Oppositions: theories on form and contrasts)
Aalborg Universitetsforlag

Friis Johansen, Karsten. 1998. Den europæiske filosofis historie. Nyt Nordisk Forlag Arnold Busk p. 62. (The history of European philosophy)

Gómez-Puerto, Gerardo et. al.. 2016. Preference for Curvature: A Historical and Conceptual Framework. Frontiers in Hum. Neuroscience, 12
January 2016 | https://doi.org/10.3389/fnhum.2015.00712

Kahneman, Daniel. 2013. Thinking, fast and slow. Farrar Straus & Giroux

Hogath, William, J. 1753. Reeves Publ.: Introdution.

Kandinsky, Wassily. 1923/26. Punkt und Linie zu Fläche. Bauhaus Bücher

Mendelsohn, Eric. 1992. Complete Works of the Architect. Princeton Architectual Press. N.Y. : p. 29

Petersen, Carl. 1920. Modsætninger. (Oppositions)
Arkitekten 1920 s. 117. København.

Rasmussen, Steen Eiler.1957. Om at opleve arkitektur. G.E.C. Gads Forlag. English version: MIT Press 1962.

Schön, Donald A. 1983. The reflective practitioner: how professionals think in action. New York

Singer, Franz.. 1923?. Note from Ittens teaching. Bauhaus Archiv. Berlin

Wilkins, A.J. Le, T.D et al.. 2017. Discomfort from urban scenes: Metabolic consequences. Publ. Landscape and Urban Planning. Volume 160, April 2017, Pages 61-68. Online version: https://www.sciencedirect.com/science/article/pii/S0169204616302699

Wölfflin, Heinrich. 1994. Classic Art, Phaidon 5.ed. London

Wölfflin, Heinrich. 1932. Principles of Art History.
Dover Publications, New York

ILLUSTRATIONS
Felicia Arvid Jaeger (F.A.J.) og Benjamin Arvid Jaeger (B.A.J.) Other photos and illustrations by the author.
Photos of Memorial to the murdered Jews of Europe by the author - with permission from P. Eisenman Architects.